Danielle Bouger

THE
DEVIL
Plays
CHESS

The Devil Plays Chess
Danielle Bouyer

©2022, Danielle Bouyer
danibouyer@gmail.com

Published by Anointed Fire House™

Edited by:
Anointed Fire House
www.anointedfirehouse.com
New Pointe Editing
www.newpointediting.com

Cover Designed by:
Anointed Fire House

ISBN: 978-1-955557-20-7

Table of Contents

Note From the Author

God put it on my heart to start writing this book earlier this year (2020). However, I had no idea how this book was going to be birthed. Finally, God gave me insight on what to write for one of the chapters. Still, after writing most of that chapter, I dealt with writer's block. So, I left the book alone for a few months, and whenever I did try to start writing again, God would say, "Don't touch that book. I don't want you writing my book in that spirit." Though I did not fully understand, I had an idea of what it was that He meant. I was still struggling with some strongholds in my life. I was also dealing with a lot of issues in my heart.

God wanted to heal me and take me through deliverance first so that I would not be writing to you as a slave, but as a free woman. I am not perfect in any way, shape, nor form. However, my mind has been completely renewed, and God is constantly taking me through a process of sanctification.

When the murder of George Floyd happened this year, I broke down crying to the Lord. I sensed the Holy Spirit telling me to fast and pray for the nation of the United States. God showed me that Satan had a red dot on the foreheads of many American citizens, and he was just waiting for an opportune time to squeeze the trigger. I was obedient to the Lord and did what He asked. I had broken down in tears during prayer because I had confessed to Him that I was weak and was not strong enough to pray and fast for an entire nation. This was not completely true because Christ has given us the authority to trample on serpents and scorpions and over all power of the adversary (Luke 10:19). However, the truth was that my prayer life was weak.

After this confession, God started to change my heart and show me that I could be and am called to be a warrior for the Kingdom. Whenever I would begin to whine during the process, He would tell me things like, "Get up" or "Stop." He would even say, "Listen, I'm not raising a wimp." God started keeping me up late at night. He had me worshiping Him and praying more and more, as well as learning certain verses and committing them to memory; these were warrior verses such as Hebrews 4:12 and Revelation 12:11. He even allowed me to be attacked in my sleep and my dreams. I realized that my Father was not babying me anymore. He would say to me, "I am training you to be a warrior." I did not understand why at first, and I would ask Him in many ways when this big war that I was supposed to fight was going to happen. But once He had finally allowed me to write this book in its entirety, I understood. The enemy attacked me in so many ways when I was writing this book. From intrusive thoughts intended to keep me bound to my past, to stomachaches, cramps, attacks during my sleep, and massive fatigue. It became more and more clear to me what my Father had been preparing me for. There was even a period when my laptop would not turn on, and I had to use my phone. All of these were attacks from the adversary; these were his attempts to discourage me.

But, because God taught me about warfare, I understood warfare. When I would be confused about some of the issues that I would face, typically when my stomach would ache, God would remind me again that it was warfare. I rejoiced in the Lord because I felt honored to go to war for Him.

This entire book is about spiritual warfare. The purpose of this book is to help and encourage believers not to be passive in their walks with Christ. God wants us to be active warriors for His Kingdom against the darkness of this world. When playing chess, to become a grandmaster, one must study the game, their opponent, and think several steps ahead of their opponent. This is the same regarding spiritual warfare, our fight against Satan, and our walk with God. Writing this book has taught me a lot and has truly blessed my life. I pray that it does the same for you as you read it. With that said, thank you for reading this book, and I hope it aids in your spiritual growth as a believer in Jesus Christ.

Chapter 1

The Game

Chess, as we all know, is a game of strategy. Those who truly understand the game know only fools or players who lack the skill, knowledge, and wisdom of playing the game make moves at random. In chess, moves must be made with intention and purpose. Furthermore, the moves should all be a part of one great and well-thought-out strategy. Failure to play the game with this approach will result in a humiliating loss, especially against a grandmaster.

According to thechessworld.com, there are five typical types of chess players: The Attack Maniac, the Passive Player, The Exchanger, The Strategist and the Perfectionist.

The Attack Maniac

This type of player plays the game with a zeal that 90%-95% of the time has no direction. They tend to haphazardly make moves that are mainly for shock value. For this type of player, the goal is to use the element of surprise to put a sudden amount of pressure on their opponent. The objective is to get the opponent to respond to their tactics and try to win the game. This kind of player is quite common in the world of chess.

The Passive Player

This type of player stays in their comfort zone during the game. Their objective is to take as many minimal risks in the game as possible; that is if they take any risks at all. This is another common type of player in chess and is the opposite of the type of player previously mentioned.

The Exchanger

This type of player takes almost every opportunity to exchange pieces with their opponent. Their agenda is to exchange their pieces until they either have a draw or a victory.

The Perfectionist

Now, it is a well-known fact that perfection is an unrealistic and unattainable goal. Yet, many of us con ourselves into believing that we can somehow make ourselves the exception to this rule and achieve the unachievable. That is the same for this type of player. They want the perfect move, the perfect game, and ultimately, the perfect win. These types of players tend to over-analyze simple moves and take prudence and caution to an unnecessary level, causing the game to be longer and more tiring than it must be. To succeed against such an opponent, a lot of tenacity, mental toughness, and patience are required.

The Strategist

This type of player is analytical as well, but with a purpose. However, they have more realistic expectations than the previously mentioned player. They do not concern themselves with making the perfect move, though they may complicate their moves at times. But it is all with a purpose. They plan and make every move with intention, while also leaving room for error and curve balls. While imperfect as well, this type of player may be one of the most esteemed types of players in the game. The evidence of this is in how everyone describes the game of chess. Statements such as, "Chess is a game of attack!" or "Chess is a game of passivity!" or "Perfection!" are rarely, if ever, made. It is commonly stated that chess is a game of strategy.

Now, the goal of this book is not to give you a chess lesson. There are plenty of courses and books on chess. Another one is not needed. The purpose is to get you, the reader, to understand how spiritual warfare should be viewed. Satan is not like your typical villain that is commonly portrayed in children's cartoons and action movies. He is not the enemy that stops for ten minutes to tell his targets and opponents about his diabolical plan. With us, rarely does he ever reveal his belligerent, bloodthirsty ways and his motives upfront. He is calculating, and his attacks are subtle, silent, intentional, and are all part of an endgame. The Devil plays chess.

So, what kind of player is Satan? Well, the answer is not in black and white. Satan understands, just like any other skilled chess player, that there is no ideal strategy. A genuinely skilled player knows that while their end goal is typically the same, to win, their game plan cannot be "one size fits all." Satan constructs his game plan and his playing style based on his opponent. Satan lurks like a predator (1 Peter 5:8); he watches his targets and studies them. So, he is always studying his opponents before deciding what angle he will attack his opponents from. Whether as a willing participant or not, the way you play chess determines the approach that Satan will take.

For example, if someone is a passive player, which most people in this world are, Satan takes more of an attack maniac approach. He attacks you with insults and negative talk from other people, mishaps, misfortunes, betrayal, crippling mindsets, such as a poverty mindset, and toxic messages from the media that can be blatant or subliminal. The endgame is always to ensure that he steals from, kills, and destroys his opponents. But his plan of how he achieves his goals are uniquely crafted for each of his opponents. For the passive opponent, the plan is to use these attacks to cause his opponent to feel an overwhelming amount of instability, discomfort, fear and even depression (which would translate as a defeatist attitude or mindset in the game of chess). These kinds of people are the ones who have the perpetual victim mentality. They are afraid to step outside of their comfort zones, which nine out of ten times would lead them to step into God's will. They stay in their comfort zones in an attempt to avoid any types of changes to their lives and lifestyles. They do not respond to changes well, whether the changes are for better or for worse. If they refuse to alter their approaches, they eventually lose the game. In life, these are the people who go into a panic when their passivity no longer serves them in any way and when everything in their lives seemingly goes left. They then become spiritually dead or physically dead; this is due to physical ailments resulting from their neglect to take care of their health because of their negative and self- sabotaging mindsets. These mindsets led them to believe that they could not do any better regarding their situations. Even worse, their physical death may even be due to them giving up on life and making the decision to end it.

Satan is a ruthless player. His goal is to defeat his opponents by any means necessary. Please, do not be deceived. Whether you are a believer of Jesus Christ or a non-believer, understand that Satan views you as his opponent. He knows that if you become victorious, you win a prize that he has been denied: eternal life. So, he would rather rob you of that prize because misery loves company, and destroy you in a game of chess. However, the only difference between him and other opponents is that once you lose against him, you will never get a rematch.

The Role You Play on the Board

In spiritual chess, you are not always an opponent. If you are not the one who Satan or any principality is directly attacking, then Satan is not interested in you being his opponent at that moment. Instead, he wants to use you as a chess piece to defeat another opponent. For example, he uses today's secular music which promotes drugs, sex, violence, and other damaging and toxic lifestyles. He also uses familiarity through familial relationships, romantic relationships, friendships, or acquaintanceships. Typically, the piece that Satan uses many of us as is a pawn. The pawn is the most disposable piece in the game. The pawns are often taken out of the game early. This happens because the person is either being used as a pawn against you for a short period or they bring harm to you while destroying themselves in the process. Either way, their time in the game as a pawn is short. In the television series, *The Wire,* written by David Simon, Ed Burns, George Pelecanos, and David Mills, D'angelo, a drug dealer explains to Wallace and Bodie, two young drug dealers who worked for him, how the game of chess is like the drug game. He also told them that the pawns whose, in this case were the drug dealers, only tickets out of the game early would be either by early retirement or, unfortunately, the more common ways: death or incarceration. This was a well-written scene in the show and arguably the most iconic scene. It foreshadowed the future of all three of the characters in this scene. But let us take it a step further; let us go deeper than the war on drugs and focus on the war for our souls.

Satan's Pawn or Yahweh's Most Powerful Piece?

Understand that we have the free will to decide how we want to live our lives, what types of players we want to be, and what kind of piece we want to be. Satan usually desires to use us as pawns to destroy others and ourselves. This solely serves him and his kingdom. It does not serve us. However, God has a desire to use us as well. But He wants to use us as His most powerful piece on the board. The queen is the chess piece with the most mobility; she is very important to the game and every chess strategist's game plan. When God uses us as this chess piece, we are to move throughout the Earth and spread His gospel. This will defeat Satan's powerful pieces, which are the principalities in his kingdom, and take the pieces (other humans) and win them over to God's Kingdom. God loves us so much that He would do anything to protect us, His valuable piece, the bride of Christ. He does this by moving through the world and protecting us against Satan's at-tacks through the use of His Holy Spirit. Also, God's end game is for all of us to be victori-ous, unlike Satan's self-serving agenda, which is to be worshiped and to eventually destroy us. So, it is up to us to decide which side of the board we want to be on.

Though Satan, as mentioned earlier, constructs his playing style and game plan based on his opponent, he is a strategist at heart. In this book, Satan's different ap-proaches to achieve his endgame and some of his "go to" strategies, such as the mirror or counterfeit strategy and the baiting strategy, will be analyzed and broken down. Becoming more aware of these strategies will help you, in addition to studying God's Word and staying in communication with Him through prayer and fasting. This will allow you to be better prepared to defeat the craftiest player in spiritual chess.

Chapter 2

The Mental Game (Master Your Mind to Defeat a Mastermind)

As warriors for Christ, we must understand our minds and exercise the dominion that God has given us over our minds. Almost everyone, if not everyone, is familiar with the saying that the game is 90% mental and 10% physical. This quote is originally from Dick Fosbury, a former professional high jumper in track and field. This is true in almost anything that we pursue. If you are not mentally fit, then you have already lost in the war of life. There is a popular African proverb that states, "If there is no enemy within, the enemy outside can do us no harm." We must battle ourselves and our flesh first so that we will not fall victim to Satan's traps and schemes. We cannot afford to be our own enemies during this time of warfare. There-fore, it is extremely important that we disci-pline our minds daily. We must let our minds know that we oversee them, and not the oth-er way around. Of course, this also applies to the game that is all about mental strategy: chess.

Secondly, we must know who our ene-my is. As stated before, Satan is a more than adept chess player. He is a grandmaster. However, too many of us act as if our oppo-nent does not exist or believe that he does not exist. Meanwhile, he is constantly mess-ing with our minds. Why? Well, if he attacks our minds first, we are at a tremendous dis-advantage before we even make our first move. Remember, he has been on this Earth for thousands of years. So, he has had much time to practice and study mankind. None of us have been on Earth as long as him, and for most of us, we have spent most of the time that we have been on Earth being ignorant to spiritual warfare.

The truth is that we cannot afford to act as if spiritual warfare does not exist. We are in this chess game, whether we are willing participants or not. So, we might as well sharpen up and learn about the game, our opponent, the team that we are on, and what positions we play. We must also be strategic. The beautiful thing for us is that God has already given us the playbook: His living Word, the Bible. It is our responsibility to study it and follow it. We have every right to win this game and no excuse to lose whatsoever.

Ways That Satan Attacks Our Minds

Fear is one of the ways that Satan attacks our minds. He can use fearful thoughts that cause us to be anxious. If we have been lazy in disciplining our minds by casting down ungodly imaginations and thoughts, and disciplining our flesh through fasting, then it is

easy for the enemy to evoke fear. As stated
before, the battle starts with us. It begins
with a decision to conquer our minds before
the enemy does. He also propagates fear
through horror movies. Too many of us are
afraid of "monsters" or dark spirits in our
homes or under our beds. It is also portrayed
in these horror movies where people are de-
picted as helpless, and the demons as powerful, and they are almost always triumphant.
They wish. Horror movies are like fantasy
movies for demons to believe that they are in
power because, in reality, they had already
lost when Jesus Christ was crucified on the
cross. For this very reason, believers who accept Jesus as their Lord and Savior are free
from the curse of the law (Galatians 3:13) and
the second death. Our issue is that we feed
into these lies sold to us by these horror films
that depict demons as having more power
than us. As a result, we tolerate these
demons. Through the blood of Jesus Christ,
we have the legal right to break any contracts

that may have been made with them in the past, and we have the legal right to stomp on them as Jesus stated when speaking to His disciples. "Behold, I have given you authority to tread on serpents and scorpions, and over all power of the enemy, and nothing shall hurt you" (Luke 10:19 ESV). The reality is that they are afraid of us. But if we do not accept Jesus Christ as our Lord and Savior, or if we give them a gateway to enter our lives through, such as horoscopes, witchcraft, and fornication, we give them a legal right to mess with us and even harm us. But know that when Satan and his troops try to psych us out in our minds by trying to appear more powerful than us, they are only bluffing. They have no real power. Their powers and abilities only fall within the bounds of what we allow and ultimately, what our Father, the Great I Am, allows.

Please take this section as a warning as well. God was ministering to me as I was lis-

17

tening to the book of Revelation. When the beast comes to Earth demanding to be worshiped, it is written that those who are for Elohim would lose their lives for not worshiping it. This also means that not everyone who will worship the beast will do it out of their heart's desire, but out of the fear of being slaughtered. If you love your life more than you love YHWH and are too attached to this Earth, Satan will be successful in scaring you into submitting to him. Do not do it. He is only as powerful as you make him, so do not make him powerful at all.

Ignorance is the second most common way that Satan defeats us in the mental game. This is not because Satan has the power to make us ignorant. Instead, it is because a lot of us choose to be ignorant. It is easy to stay in our comfort zones, but ladies and gentlemen, we are in a war. We cannot afford to be ignorant of our authority and the power that we have through Jesus Christ, nor can we be ignorant of the attacks and common strategies of our adversary. The answers are in the Bible. The revelation and understanding of these answers come through prayer and spending time with our Father.

How the Devil Almost Beat Me in Chess

One of my biggest struggles was not conquering my mind. My issue was not casting down fantasies, which I will detail later in this book. I have had other struggles such as pride, lust, laziness, and unforgiveness. However, it would always start with a fantasy. The grace of Christ Jesus is why I am even able to focus and write this entire book. I was a maladaptive daydreamer. Maladaptive daydreaming is a condition or habit of daydreaming excessively; it could include acting out the daydream verbally, physically, or both. I was an extreme fantasizer who would even act out the daydreams. I had a lot of great ideas but would never put them into action. I always settled for the instant gratification that would come through pretending that my fantasies had already taken place, instead of putting in the work to make them happen. This includes a lot of work that I wanted to do for God, work I felt that He was inspiring me to do. When I would get out of my head and return to reality, I would find myself in the same position with the same problems that I'd tried to escape by daydreaming. It eventually led me into a deep depression, and I had even entertained the idea of taking my life. It was my faith and my belief in Jesus Christ that prevented me from executing this heinous act. Praise God! He delivered me from this depressing cycle once I was finally ready to stop playing tug of war with Him, and I let Him take full control of my life. Is the temptation still there? Yes. But the blood of Jesus is greater. Therefore, I do not have to bow to those demons. They have already been conquered for me. Satan played a game with my mind through maladaptive daydreaming. Just imagine if he had succeeded. I would not have

been able to do the work that I do for Christ
today.

Though this might come across as
strange, I thank God for that 20-year struggle. Yes, 20 years. Had it not been for that
struggle, my life would have probably been
great and more fulfilling, or at least appear to
be. Then, I probably would have felt as if I did
not need Him. I searched and searched for
answers, but this condition remains under-
studied and misunderstood by most. Thankfully, Christ Jesus was and is the only answer
that makes sense for me. The only cure that
works. I am truly free because of Him.

Chapter 3

The Pieces of the Board

As mentioned in the introduction, we can easily become pawns on the board for Satan to use during this war. But what are his other pieces? The other pieces in a chess game are the bishop, the knight, the rook, the queen, and the king. There are eight pawns: two bishops, two rooks, two knights, one queen, and one king on the board.

So, if most humans are pawns for Satan, who are the other pieces? Demonic principalities are the equivalency of the pieces that are behind the pawns. Pawns typically do the dirty work, and they are disposable. The average chess player doesn't lose much sweat when he or she loses a pawn.

When a person operating under Satan's influence does his dirt, neither Satan nor his principalities show any signs of concern for the individual when their actions cause them death, jail time, or a trip down the road of in-sanity. But if that individual should receive deliverance and the demons that influence them are attacked, you usually hear those demons cry before they are cast out. In other words, Satan is saying, "No! You have hit one of my important pieces on the board!" This can even happen when you call out a spirit that one is operating in. That person would either become overly defensive, or they may go on a tirade with the intent of dragging your name through the mud. These actions are another example of the demon or princi-pality crying because they have been hit.

The major pieces on Satan's side of the board depends on what strategy he is using in that moment. The Jezebel spirit or principali-ty can be used and will be discussed in further examples as we continue to discuss Satan's strategies in this book. Another major spirit that Satan uses is the spirit of bondage. This is equivalent to the strategy of chess players who study their opponents; these players take notes of their opponents' positions or weaknesses. They then exploit those weaknesses. Essentially, once any piece is moved out of its position, there will be at least one area of weakness. Even when a player gambits a pawn, (typically white) using the Tennison Gambit to bait the opponent's more powerful pieces, an area of weakness will be created. Before going in-depth about how Satan uses certain plays against us and how this relates to chess, it is important to discuss the function of each of the pieces in the game.

The Pawn

Each player has eight pawns in the game. The pawns are on the front line, and their function is to protect or cover for the pieces behind them. Their function is also, a lot of the time, to be sacrificed for baiting the opponent; they do this to obtain one of their opponent's most important pieces or to carry out any other strategy that will help the player win the game.

**Pawn Promotion

Pawn promotion is when a pawn reaches the end of the opponent's side of the board and gets promoted to a higher rank. This could be a bishop, rook, knight, or queen, but not a king, as in the game, there can only be one king for each player on the board. No one else can become a king. Satan would rarely do this unless one of his pawns is extremely bound by a spirit that would cause them to be an infiltrator in God's Kingdom. For example, someone bound by a seducing spirit can be used by Satan to get into the church and discourage a potential soul from being led to Christ due to their ungodly behavior. This is sometimes what happens when someone leaves the church because they have seen many hypocritical behaviors from the people in the church. While this hypocrisy could be due to someone lacking knowledge of the faith and God's Word, Satan can also use a pawn to make a mockery of God in His church, causing people to fall away from the faith. While it is true that God's grace can save anyone who enters a church, some people do not want to be saved and are being used, whether knowingly or unknowingly, by Satan to be promoted in the game. When Satan's pawn successfully enters the church, gets involved in the church, moves up in rank in the church, and then corrupts the church and its image, Satan sees this as his pawn successfully reaching the end of his opponent's side of the board. This typically results in scandals that cause the church to be viewed in a negative light. So, always remember that not everyone in the church is operating under the spirit of Christ, and that some of them have no intentions of being saved. This is the reality of the game.

The Rook, the Knight, and the Bishop

There are two of each of these pieces for each player in the game. Their function is to protect the king. They do what the pawns cannot do, and they do what the queen does not have to do. They are the equivalent of the middle managers of a facility or a corporation that can either have a tyrannical nature and breathe down your neck at a job (the ungodly spirits), or they are the ones that inspire you to perform at your highest level through motivation, encouragement, guidance and leading by example (the godly spirits). They are the overseers.

While these are not the most powerful pieces on the board, they are still quite effective in doing damage. This makes them a significant threat to the opponent.

The Queen

There is one queen for each opponent. The queen is the most powerful piece on the board. This piece's primary function is to protect the king. The use of the queen in the game can give the player a lot of mobility and power in the game. However, the player is in the most vulnerable state when using the queen because the involvement of the queen in the game also puts the player at risk of losing the queen. Once the queen is lost, a lot of power is lost, and a great amount of protection for the king is lost.

The King

There is one king for each player on the board. The most important piece of the game is the king. The king is not required to make a lot of moves, nor is it able to. The king's business is to stay in position and rule the kingdom. If the king is captured, the player who lost the king automatically loses the game. This is known as checkmate. So, what is the king in your life? What is it that Satan can take from you to end you? It is your salvation, your soul, and your relationship with Jesus Christ. These are things that you should treat as your king on the board, and you must guard them with your life.

Passive Pieces vs. Active Pieces

Passive pieces are pieces that are not in any position to attack and generally do not pose a threat to the opponent's pieces, whereas, active pieces are able to attack the opponent's pieces. There are active and passive pieces in God's Kingdom, just as there are active and passive pieces in Satan's kingdom. There are some churches that tend to be very passive; they worship, have a dead service, and then go home. They do not even bother to spread the Word of God or the good news.

There are also passive people in the church who do not grow in their faith; they go to church services as if they are Sunday concerts followed by lectures. They do not invite anyone to their churches, and the lessons they learn seem to not affect them because their spirits are dead. As believers, we must be mindful of this and avoid being passive. Active churches and members of the church are proactively involved in spiritual warfare and pose a great threat to Satan. Satan also has passive pieces as well. These are typically his pawns or non-believers who are influenced by dark spirits that have not yet manifested. These are also familiar spirits that we may have been delivered from that lurk and wait for a door to open; these spirits are very patient. It is important that we do not sleep on Satan's passive pieces.

Satan will never sleep on God's passive pieces either. He does anything in his power to draw them away from God's Kingdom or keep them in that passive state. He will even attack and capture them because he knows just how easily and how quickly they can become a threat if they wake up.

The Points and Value of Each Piece
- **Pawn: 1 point**
- **Knight: 3 points**
- **Bishop: 3 points**
- **Rook: 5 points**
- **Queen: 9 points**
- **King: You cannot put a number on the value of the king!**

When you are on God's side, you have the highest value just under the king as the queen. When you are on Satan's side, you have the lowest value as the pawn. You can increase in rank as this does happen in the game, like becoming a minister for Satan's kingdom, for example, which would be the equivalent of a pawn being promoted to the bishop on the board. However, bear in mind that Satan, overall, views his pieces, especially if they are pawns, as disposable.

When God is the Player

When God is the player, He is the ultimate strategist. No piece is insignificant in His eyes. Each piece, from the greatest to the least in rank, has value and is precious to Him. It is for this reason that He is intentional about every single move that He makes. This has been God's method since the beginning of time. The pawns are the seeds of the gospel that are planted to help attract the attention of non- believers. The purpose of these seeds is to lead non- believers to salvation, which would cause them to join the side of God. Examples would be songs, conversations, movies, or even a simple word of encouragement. These seeds function as pawns because, while important, they can be taken out of the game early and die if Satan uses a strategy that causes the death of these seeds. They are also used to draw in the opposition with the intent of causing them to join the side of Christ. Jesus even mentions the planting of these seeds to His disciples.

Then He told them many things in parables saying: "A farmer went out to sow his seed. As he was scattering the seed, some fell along the path, and the birds came and ate it up. Some fell on rocky places, where it did not have much soil. It sprang up quickly, be-cause the soil was shallow. But when the sun came up, the plants were scorched and with-ered because they had no root. Other seeds fell among thorns, which grew up and choked the plants. Still other seed fell on good soil, where it produced a crop- a hundred, sixty or thirty times what was sown" (Matthew 13:3-8 NIV).

The plants being scorched, choked, and eaten by birds are examples of the pawns getting taken by the opposition. This does not stop the gospel from reaching thousands and hundreds of thousands, however. Just as one or a few pawns taken do not stop the game's flow, nor does it stop the player's chance of winning.

The rook is the Holy Spirit (as mentioned before, there are two rooks but only one Holy Spirit). However, to demonstrate how the Kingdom works in this example, the rook will be referred to as a single piece. The Holy Spirit and the rook function the same way (as it will be shown in further examples). The bishops are the ministers and leaders of God's Kingdom, and the knights are the angels who God has sent to guard us. They protect us from harm and they protect God's church. They are the messengers and warriors of God, and while they are not the highest in rank in the Kingdom, they still pose a great threat to Satan and his kingdom.

The queen is the church. Why is the church like the most powerful piece on the board? Well, look at the task that we have before us. Our job is to defend the Word and spread the Word. We have the most mobility in this Earth. We can physically spread and plant seeds of the gospel. Not to mention, when a believer in the church is lost, it hurts God, the player, severely. Many people talk about how Judas, the first apostate known in history, betrayed Jesus Christ. Many focus on his greed, wickedness and disloyalty. Many also point out that Jesus was able to foresee this betrayal. However, not many mention how deeply this must have hurt Jesus emotionally. Just imagine someone who you have allowed to walk with you, someone you have appointed as one of your disciples, which is a very important position (it is the same as the queen on the board), has turned around and stabbed you in the back. But a skilled chess player like God understands that it is okay to lose your queen when carrying out an overall strategy. This is because you know that you can get it back later in the game. Judas' betrayal and Peter's denial of his relation to Christ were all a part of a plan that needed to be fulfilled. It was a plan that led to hundreds of thousands of believers being added to the church. God got His queen back through pawn promotion. He did this by using the gospel (His pawn) and promoting it to queen status. He did this by building the church on the foundation of the gospel. She came back stronger than ever, and she is the biggest threat to Satan and his kingdom. As stated earlier, we must remember that the queen is also vulnerable when being used in the game. Satan is desperate to get his hands on God's queen. He knows that if he can take the queen, he can get closer to the king. Look at some of the churches today. Some churches have a very worldly influence, and who is the prince of the world? Satan. Unfortunately, Satan is working on taking God's queen. Therefore, we must continue to stay in the position that God has placed us in, as well as continuing to study and educate ourselves on God's Word and the opposition. So many churches and believers in the church are not operating as God's most powerful piece on the board. We can't even cast out demons. This scares them, and so does the name of

Jesus. We have no need to fear nor submit to Satan and his principalities. They fear us because they are familiar with the team that we play for and they know our Father's capability of inflicting serious damage. The second chapter discussed how dangerous it could be if you allowed your opponent to be more aware of your weaknesses than you are. But it is also just as bad if you allow your opponent to be more aware of your strengths than you are.

Lastly, the king is Jesus. He is the most important piece on the board. Without Jesus, the game would be over, and there would be no salvation. The king is currently in position on the throne in the Kingdom of Heaven. He is coming back to get physically involved in the game again, and when He does, it will be game over for the adversary.

When Satan is the Player

Satan is strategic as well and is not to be underestimated. He, like God, is intentional about his moves. But before addressing his moves and strategies, we must first understand the pieces on his side of the board and their functions.

The people of the world, those who don't serve God, are Satan's pawns. Satan uses his pawns as pieces to be sacrificed to further his agenda. He uses pawns to bait the pieces from God's side—mainly God's queen, the church. An example of Satan baiting one of God's pieces was when the religious officials searched for Jesus to kill Him and received the information from Judas by offering him compensation. Satan took Judas from God's side by using money and the religious officials, his pawns, and then used him also as a pawn to get to the king, Jesus. But once Satan was finished with him, he drove him to his death. This was done by Satan doing another

thing that he does best—being the great ac-
cuser. Judas became guilt-ridden when he
learned that Jesus was going to be crucified;
he committed suicide once he was unable to
give the money back to the Pharisees and go
back on their deal. This is how Satan treats
his pawns. They do the job that he wants, and
once he is finished with them, he disposes of
them.

Think about a time when someone said
or did something that completely spoiled your
day. This may have caused you to feel great
sadness or it may have even caused you to
act out of character. You may then start to
feel contempt for that person, causing you to
walk in one of the most crippling spirits: the
spirit of unforgiveness. But what happened in
this situation? Satan used one of his pawns to
bait you. *"For our struggle is not against
flesh and blood, but against the authorities,
against the powers of this dark world and
against the spiritual forces of evil in the*

heavenly realms" (Ephesians 6:12 NIV). Bear this in mind so that you will not be baited and become Satan's pawn too.

Another example of this is a common bad judgment call that believers make. This is being unequally yoked with non-believers. It is never an accident when a non-believer comes into a believer's life. This could be in a friendship, romantic relationship, and even in some cases, a business relationship. This move is another way for Satan to bait a believer. *"Can two walk together except they be agreed?"* (Amos 3:3 KJV). In this case, one is bound to be influenced by the other. If this is the position that God has placed you in, chances are you will be immovable. You will influence the non-believer and he or she will most likely give his or her life to Christ. But if it is a situation where you have been baited out of your position, and this was not God's doing, you may become influenced by the non-believer. You may start to worship other

deities, that individual, or worst of all, yourself. Worshiping yourself is the worst of all
because it is a manifestation of pride, which
is one of the seven deadly sins. But no matter
what you choose to worship at that point, you
are still following Satan. There is no gray area
with God. Either you are with Him, or you are
against Him. This is not to say that you cannot have an encounter with a non-believer.
How else can a believer witness? However,
you must stay submitted to God and only
witness to the non-believer—nothing else.
Many believers make the mistake of dancing
with the non-believer, only for that person to
trip them on the dance floor, causing them to
fall.

The bishops are ministers and leaders
in Satan's kingdom. The knights are the demonic spirits that serve Satan. The rooks are
the demonic principalities that have dominion
over the demonic spirits. Just as the rook
ranks higher than the knight, demonic princi-

palities rank higher than demons. This will be further discussed later in the book when each pieces' moves are analyzed. As mentioned earlier, just as the bishops, knights, and rooks are behind the pawns in the game, Satan's leaders (demonic spirits and principalities) are behind the people they influence: Satan's pawns.

So, who or what is Satan's queen? What has the most moves on Satan's side of the board? Pride. Pride is behind this entire war that Satan has declared against God. Satan knows that he will lose, but his pride will not allow him to give it a rest. Satan's pride is behind all the pieces that were previously mentioned. Pride also has a lot of moving power. It has moved so far in this world that it has infected most of humanity. This is evident in today's climate. So many people are walking in pride. Out of all the seven deadly sins, pride is the most lethal because it takes a great deal of pride to commit the other deadly sins, or any sin, for that matter, and defy God. You know the consequences deep down in your heart because God has given all of us a moral compass—no exceptions. However, many people today still commit these sins. Pride causes them to create nonsensical arguments to defend their perverse actions. While the lust for God's power caused Adam and Eve to want to eat the fruit of the forbidden tree, pride is what gave them the nerve to do so. Pride is what got Satan cast out of Heaven. Pride, like the queen, can do and has done a lot of damage. But also, like the queen, when it is used, it is very vulnerable. It is fragile. The saying "a hit dog will holler" apropos this fact. An example of this is when a pastor is giving a sermon and makes a general statement. The people who walk in pride are convinced that the pastor is referring to them, and they make it their mission to defend their pride. Whether or not the pastor knows them personally is beside the point. In their minds, everyone knows who

they are, and because their pride is so sensi-
tive and so vulnerable, the pawn must fight to
protect it at all costs.

So, who or what are these pieces all
protecting? Who or what is the king? Satan's
king is his kingdom. His kingdom has its doctrines and principles. If his king is lost and no
longer influences the world, he is finished.

Chapter 4

The Opening Game

The opening game is just as it sounds; it is the start of the game. The best approach is to aim for the center of the board. This is because it puts your pieces in a more active position. The center of the board will be discussed more in-depth in chapter ten. A skilled chess player would not allow his or her opponent to dominate the center of the board. But placing your pawns and pieces at the center of the board or as close to the center of the board as possible is typically the best way to open in the game.

You would want to avoid opening along the files (all the squares in a vertical line) at the most outer part of the board. This would put your pieces in a less active position,

making it more difficult for them to attack.
This is the equivalent of believers who stay
outside of church homes and prayer groups
where they can be more active in God's Kingdom. This does not mean that they are not
saved. They are just not as active in the
Kingdom when they walk with Christ as lon-
ers. God will have you in a season like this
when He wants to reveal something to you or
develop you, which will be discussed in more
detail later in this chapter. When you are
staying outside of the church or any fellowship groups due to "church hurt," you are
hindering your growth and are an easier target for Satan. In a situation like this, it is best
to pray about the offense to gain clarity. If it
was blatant disrespect on that member's part,
then respectfully speak to that individual first
(Matthew 18:15). If the situation is not re-
solved after the discussion or attempted discussion, then go to a leader. If you were offended by a leader, go to that leader's leader.
If you have tried to resolve the issue within

the church and were unsuccessful, pray that God would help you to find another church home. Also, bear in mind that sometimes, simple correction may seem like an offense to those walking in pride or are not used to having order or being corrected. Also, contrary to popular belief, most offenses are unintentional. So, a simple conversation and some clarity will usually lead to a resolution.

Another reason believers "play the edge of the board" by staying outside of church homes or fellowship groups is because they feel that they are not "holy enough." This was my struggle during the first two years of my walk with Christ. My parents kept trying to encourage me to go to the youth meeting at my church, but like the average teen, I was super self-conscious and knew that I was constantly stumbling in my walk. Therefore, I felt that I was not good enough to attend. I was greatly deceived. When I finally decided to go, there was no judgment, and everyone was really welcoming. It helped me to grow stronger in my walk. So, just a word of advice to anyone who is "church shy" or has "fellowship-phobia," you will never be good enough. But neither will any of the members that you are having fellowship with. Therefore, we need to be with other believers to support us, and we need Christ to sanctify us. Satan prefers when God's pieces are standing along the outer file of the board because there is strength in numbers. Pieces at the center or close to the center of the board have a better chance of supporting each other and are closer to where the action happens; this makes God's Kingdom a great threat to Satan's kingdom.

Another method that most chess players use in the opening of the game is developing their pieces. These pieces may not be fully active, but they are being prepared for battle. These are newly born-again Christians, deliverance ministers in training, pastors in training, or a group of believers pre-paring to go on a missionary trip.

The opening sets the tone for the game. A bad opening can be costly, but not completely detrimental. Players can have a bad or mediocre opening, but if they spend enough time analyzing their mistakes, the board, their opportunities, their opponent's moves and potential mistakes, and their op-ponent's opportunities, they can strategize a strong comeback in the middle and endgame where the points count. So, if your opening (the way that your life started before you knew Christ or at the beginning of your walk with Christ) was not the best, either because of something you did or something another person did, do not fret. Stay with God and study His Word, analyze your mistakes, and improve your game because the game is not yet over.

Chapter 5

The Middle Game

The middle game is the heart of the game. This is when threats are made, threats are answered, strategies of both parties are unfolding, and pieces are captured. It is also where most of each of the players' points are made. This is where one's skill, patience, and ability to control the game are exposed. Some people start with killer openings, but then play as if they are first-timers who have no knowledge of the game during their middle or end games. Therefore, it is important to continuously study and gain knowledge of the game, in addition to developing your strategies for your opening, middle, and end game.

This is what Satan does. He constantly studies God and the world, both believers and non-believers, and he uses the knowledge that he gains to continually develop and improve his strategy. His opening game with Adam and Eve was strong; it set the tone for the entire game. His middle game was rather weak compared to God's middle game when He sent Jesus (our King), down to Earth. He then did a castling move, which will be discussed in a later chapter, with the rook (the Holy Spirit), when Jesus went to Heaven and put the Holy Spirit in a more active position in the game so that He could work with the queen (the church). We are now in the endgame, and Satan is desperately pulling out all his best moves. He has been successful at deceiving many.

But how does this relate to believers individually? Well, when we get saved and give our lives over to Christ, it is important that we make sure that we do not start out as those overzealous Christians who have a strong opening game but decline in our passion and faith by the middle game. This commonly happens when believers do not study the Word of God fervently and do not focus on their strengths and weaknesses. Satan, our opponent, is doing this without rest. Therefore, we must continue to study, gain knowledge, and develop strategies to avoid falling into temptation. We must also use our strengths to our advantage and develop in the areas that we are weak. For example, some people are great with prayer and interceding for others but are weak at evangelizing or engaging in fellowship. Another example would be where Satan can tempt us. For some, addiction may not be a stronghold, but pride and religiousness may be where they are weak and bound. It is important that we:

- keep our eyes open
- always have a heart to grow and increase in our faith
- have a heart for God.

This way, we fight just as hard, if not harder, than Satan's kingdom.

But we must not make moves haphazardly. We must make our moves with a purpose. We must exercise wisdom when studying and sharing the Word of God. Two of the major mistakes are not understanding that there is a time and place for everything (Ecclesiastes 3) and casting our pearls before swine (Matthew 7:6). An example of the first major mistake and waste of a move would be speaking in tongues when there is no interpreter present (1 Corinthians 14:28). Doing this would leave other believers and non-believers in the dark. If there is no interpreter, who are you ministering to? Who are you blessing? This is an example of wasting a move. This could have been an opportunity to bless someone, but that very same person may be confused and discouraged, and it may even cause the individual to leave the church, especially if he or she is a non-believer.

An example of the second major mistake that many believers make is trying to convince someone that Jesus Christ exists when they have their minds completely made up that He does not. They may even proceed to argue with them. But even Jesus said to His disciples, "If anyone will not welcome you or listen to your words, shake the dust off your feet when you leave that home or town" (Matthew 10:14 NIV). This would also be a waste of a move. Instead, show them who Christ is through your behavior. This way, if you do not win them over, you may win over another individual or several individuals who may be watching you. Be strategic and be intentional with every move that you make because the souls of this world depend on it. The next few chapters will be the types of strategies Satan has been using and will continue to use in the middle game of spiritual chess.

Chapter 6

The Baiting Strategy

I watched a video by a YouTuber named Dre Baldwin who talked about the game of chess. I did not know too much about the game and had only played once and sur- prisingly won. But I did not try to learn about the game more in-depth and build upon whatever little skill I had gained at the time. So, I decided to watch an introductory video that would help to refresh my memory on whatever I had learned about the game a few years prior, as well as break down the basics. I did this so that if I had ever decided to play again, I would not be going into the game blindly or leaning on beginner's luck once again.

But Baldwin mentioned a type of player that stood out to me. He said "a Machiavellian type of individual." He described this type of individual as someone who dangles a shiny object to attract a foolish or gullible individual. Once this individual takes the bait, they fall into a very hard trap for them to redeem themselves from. This is a baiting strategy, and it is the first recorded strategy that Satan used in the Bible. This strategy is illustrated in the story of Adam and Eve in the book of Genesis. Satan read his opponent, Adam, and saw that he had the desire to be like God. He also knew that Eve had the same desire but would be more fit to be a pawn against Adam. Yes, it is true that Satan tempted both Adam and Eve to eat from the Tree of the Knowledge of Good and Evil. He did this by deceiving Eve and tempting her with the promise that she'd be her own king. However, to fall into agreement with sin and disobedience, the desire and curiosity had to have already been inside of an individual. Satan knew that Adam was left in charge of the Garden of Eden, so he was the target. Unfortunately, Satan understood more than Adam did that the one in power would have a greater fall, a greater measure of responsibility and be held more accountable than the individual he had dominion over.

In this case, the shiny dangling object was the idea of being like the almighty, all-seeing, and all-knowing God. Satan saw both Adam and Eve's lust for God's power living inside of them. How could he not? He knew that form of lust all too well. It was the very same reason why he was cast out of Heaven. So, because he saw the very trait he possessed lurking in Adam and Eve, he knew how to play them both by using Eve as a pawn to swindle Adam out of his position of power. Before this happened, Adam had the upper hand in the game. The problem was that Adam was not aware of his great advantage over Satan. Adam did not know that his own counterpart was being used as a pawn against him to persuade him to submit to his fleshly desire and disobey God. To be honest, Adam did not need to have this knowledge if he would have just listened to God's instruction. But he was not the passive type of player. He was an exchanger. So, he thought that he could exchange his obedience to God and his life for an opportunity to "be like God," which seemed like a grand opportunity at the time. But it was merely a dangling shiny object that led him and Eve into a trap that cost him the win and gave Satan the upper hand.

What Baldwin meant by "a Machiavellian type of individual" is that they are as cunning as Satan was to Adam and Eve. Niccolo Machiavelli is known for his works, *The Prince*, *The Art of War* (not to be confused with Sun Tzu's *The Art of War*), and *Discourses on Livy* with *The Prince* being the most popular. In Machiavelli's, *The Prince*, he discusses methods and ways for principalities to stay in power through manipulation. These manipulation tactics can be as subtle and covert as allying with other nations simply to have the upper hand in the war and in leadership, or they may be as overt and ruthless as making an example out of one of your enemies by beheading them in front of a public audience. This was a common practice in those times.

Satan uses these same practices either directly or, even more commonly, through the principalities of his dark kingdom. An example of a well-known but sometimes misunderstood devil is the principality called Jezebel. It is a common misconception that Jezebel, and the women that are influenced by this spirit, dwell and dance in the realm of whoredom and sensual or sexual seduction. However, while these traits are apropos to the Jezebel principality, these are merely tools to help this dark and demonic spirit gain what it wants: ungodly authority. Jezebel is not just the whore trying to lead you into fornication. But it is, in a lot of cases, invited in through fornication as well as rebellion. This spirit is not only found in women but is also found in men as well. It is invited into our lives when we are out of order: God's order. This is a good principality to study so that you are aware of it and not blindsided by it, as it is running rampant in society today. I recommend Tiffany Buckner's YouTube video, *Unmasking The Jezebel Spirit, and* her books, *Jezebellion* (parts one and two), coupled with the actual story of Ahab and Jezebel found in 1 Kings 16 for starters, which will also be examined further in chapter 8 when discussing false prophets.

Jezebel is a move that Satan has used for a long time. He will continue to use this move, as revealed in Revelation 2:20, because it works for him. Many of his opponents are completely blindsided by this move; they do not realize how this very cunning and sly strategy has been used against them until it is too late and the Devil has already won. This move goes hand-in-hand with the Machiavellian or baiting strategy. Both Jezebel and Machiavelli believed in control and obtaining what one wants by any means necessary. They also both believed in doing almost everything with ulterior motives. For the Jezebel move to work, opponents must first get out of their rightful positions. However, it is quite rare that anyone would voluntarily and willingly give up his or her position, especially if it means taking that individual off the path to victory; that is unless the player is using it as a baiting tactic. So, how do you get your opponents to give up their positions? The same way that the serpent got Adam and Eve to give up their positions; he dangled a shiny object. The shiny object usually comes in the form of whatever the opponent's fleshly desire is: money, more power, less work, glory, admiration, etc. But as Baldwin mentioned in his comprehensive video, when your opponent presents an opportunity for you that is too good to be true, chances are, it is. This is assuming that your opponent is a master of the game and not a novice, which should always be considered. Once we take the bait and reach for the shiny object, we focus on our seemingly significant gain while disregarding the fact that we have now left certain pieces on the board exposed because we are no longer able to keep them protected.

Spiritually speaking, when Satan baits us, and we take the bait by going toward it and grabbing it, we step out of position with God. We then focus on our small, fleshly, evanescent gain and take our attention off what we now risk losing: our peace, sound minds, joy, our Christ-like spirituality, our relationship with Christ, and even our lives. These are all more valuable pieces on our board than whatever cheap piece that Satan has baited us into pursuing.

A common way that this happens, especially in western society, is that women tend to step out of their positions as women. The bait that they usually go toward is the idea of controlling or being in charge of their households which, at first, seems like a great exchange. Femininity and being the head of a household do not go well together, not because it is impossible, but because it requires more masculine energy. Therefore, a woman would have to exchange her natural position as a feminine woman to step into a more manly role. This later leads to stress and mental strain that a woman is just not designed for. A woman is designed to nurture (mainly her children and herself), submit to her husband if she is married, and live in her femininity. However, Satan has gotten the modern-day woman to step out of her position. In chess, if your opponent has baited you to get your pieces out of their rightful positions, you leave your valuable pieces exposed. Also, in chess, if your opponent can get to your queen, it is a high chance that they will get your king as well. Hence, you will lose the game. Just as in the case of Adam and Eve, Satan knew that if he could get to the queen, he would have a better shot at getting to the king. Women have a God-given, soft, sensual, and persuasive nature that has the power to break down a man's hard armor; it also helps to facilitate an atmosphere of peace. This gentle nature was given to a woman by God so that she can be open to receive wisdom from God; this way she could nurture, heal and support her family. Her male counterpart, if willing, can pull that God-given wisdom out of her to make him a better and stronger man in Christ. These characteristics used in a godly way will make a woman into the type of wife described in Proverbs 31. However, Satan sometimes uses the nature of a woman against her and men to disrupt God's order, and to get men out of their rightful positions with God. A great example of this is in the case of Samson and

Delilah in Judges 16. A woman can be a man's healer if used by God, but a man's kryptonite if used by Satan.

A lot of men today, unfortunately, walk around not knowing their roles and who they were called to be in Christ Jesus. They also are very confused about their identities and their roles as men. Also, some men are very passive and effeminate. Furthermore, some men desire to be women and may even go the extra mile to physically become a woman. This results from Satan utilizing the Jezebel principality and the baiting strategy to break down his opponents.

How do we avoid falling victim to this strategy?

The number one way to not fall prey to such a deceiving tactic is to stay in position. A skilled chess player knows not to be reactive, but strategic. Always assume that your opponent is a skilled chess player which, in this case, he is. Also, always assume that every move is made purposely to set you up for failure. Any move that the opponent makes may seem simple or stupid, but a skilled chess player knows if it is too good to be true. So, they wait, study the board, and strategize to make a wise move that will keep their most valuable pieces in positions that are advantageous for the player. For example, a player can put their knight in the path of your rook.

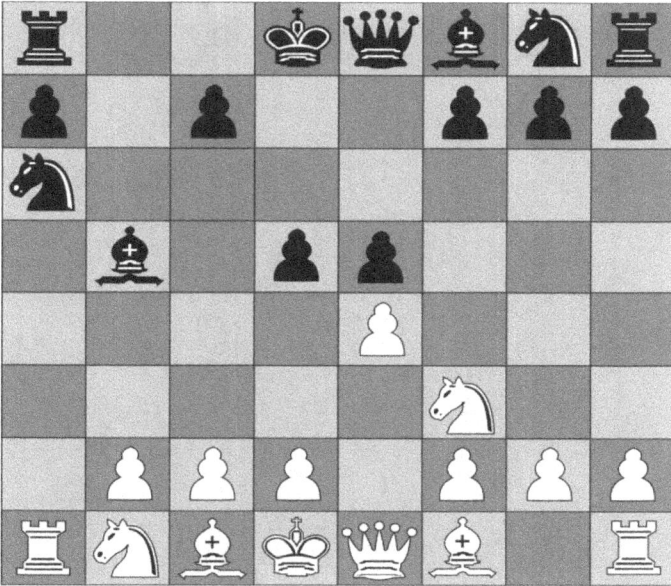

White's rook can move vertically and capture black's knight.

Your first instinct may be to capture their knight. But as you analyze the board further, you notice that once your rook lands in the position of where their knight is, you will be directly in the path of their bishop and pawn.

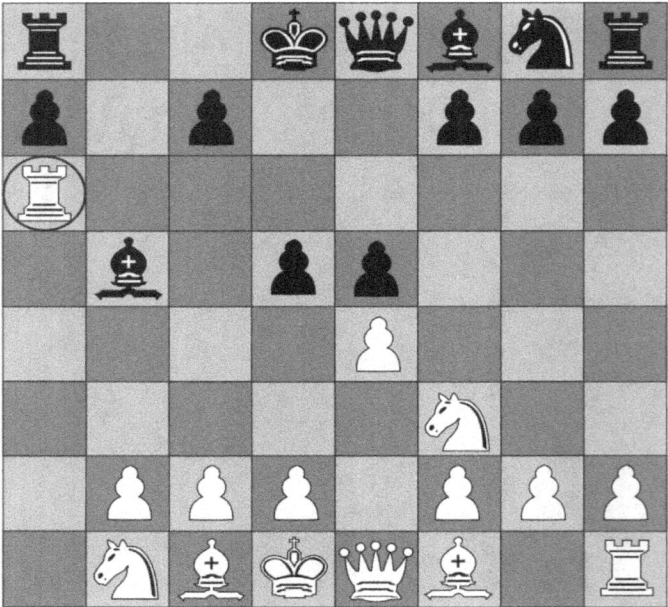

White's rook is now in the path of black's pawn and bishop.

Is it worth it? Absolutely not! Your rook is worth five points, and their knight and bishop are only worth three. Their pawn is only worth one point. Therefore, if you allow your rook to be captured, you will lose a more valuable piece than the knight that you captured. This is the equivalent of us risking something of ours that is of value, such as eternal life, to capture one or more of Satan's petty promises—promises of this world that will soon perish.

Satan can and will often make a move that, at first glance, would appear to be in our favor. However, we must not be hasty. Instead, we must think like skilled chess players. We must wait, analyze the circumstance, study the Bible, listen out for God's voice, and stay in position!

One of the greatest examples of how many people in society, including believers, have stepped out of position with God is the normalization of sexual immorality. Satan knows our weak spots. Every chess player has a weak area and should be aware of their vulnerable areas on the board, as well as their opponent's vulnerable areas. Our weakest area is our flesh. Satan knows this, and so does God. God commands us through His Word to not give in to our fleshly desires; this is to protect us. Satan, however, uses this knowledge and exploits it by using the baiting strategy to attack us where we are weak. Just as Satan lied to Eve, Satan told this nation the biggest lie that has affected us for generations and sadly, will continue to affect us for generations to come. This lie was that anything goes, and we can do whatever we want without reaping the consequences. Or, at least, not the consequences that are stated in the Bible.

The most common lies today include the illusion of sexual freedom, age, and gender. People even lie when they say, for example, "Whether you are in a marriage or committed relationship does not matter. It's your body! You have every right to do what you want with it, and you do not have to submit to an imaginary 'genie in the sky' or a book that was written by man, designed to control the masses." It is true that it is your body and you do not have to submit to a higher power if you choose not to, but whether you believe that there is a God or not is irrelevant. The fact of the matter is that there is a God, and his name is Yahushua. He has paid the price for this very sin, as well as other sins so that we may be forgiven and saved. But we must get in position and stay in position. You can do whatever it is that you want to do with your body. You can give your body to whoever it is that you want to give it to. But understand that you will always reap what you sow. Broken families, single-parent homes, a generation growing up with confusion about their identities, ungodly soul ties, and sexually transmitted diseases are all results of the normalization and aggressive promotion of sexual immorality, whether we want to accept it or not.

So, as believers, what strategy can we use to combat this destructive move that Satan has made against us? First, you must be aware of where you are strong and where you are weak. Too often is Satan more aware of our strengths and weaknesses than we are. Do not have too much confidence in yourself. A believer's confidence should be placed in God and only in God. So, start with God. Start your day talking to Him and listening to Him. You do this by having moments of silence and fully being in His presence, reading His Word, and meditating on His Word. Next, ask God to expose where you are weak. After this, find a way to strengthen that area. Here is an example: Tom wakes up every morning and places his phone on airplane mode. *Why?* So that he has no distractions and can spend time starting his day with God. *Why?* Because he understands that his most powerful position is when he is in submission to God. *What kind of distractions is Tom trying to avoid?* Going on Instagram. *Why?* Because of the Instagram models that reveal their bodies. *Why?* Because he falls into lust when looking at them. *So what?* Falling into lust causes him to then go on certain websites to find certain "stars" who resemble those Instagram models. *So, that won't hurt him; right?* Wrong. Tom understands that he can open himself up even further to engage in fornication, especially with his neighbor who has been inviting him over for about a year and has been overly flirtatious with him. She too resembles those Instagram models. He also understands that she has two children out of wedlock, and he could potentially give her a third. This would be a burden that he would have to deal with for the rest of his life. He understands that she has a reputation for causing chaos in the lives of the other two children's fathers, and she has no intentions of becoming a wife because she wants to stay on the market and relish in the attention that she receives for her body. Therefore, Tom has blocked her and his favorite Instagram models. His friends think that these are extreme moves on his part, nevertheless, regardless of what they say, he still puts his phone on airplane mode in the morning. He even prays that he has the strength to not unblock those models and his neighbor with the intent of looking at their photo galleries. Tom uses his Instagram to promote his ministry for God, which is why he has not deleted it. But Tom has made it up in his heart that if he must delete the app, he will. Nevertheless, this is not all that there is to Tom's strategy. He understands his weakness and how far he has come from sexual sin. He is also aware that he can fall back into it. Therefore, he is working two jobs and saving his money to build a website to bring his current audience away from Instagram. He is also saving money to hire a Christian social media marketing expert to oversee his Instagram. Tom will then no longer have access to his Instagram because the expert will push his ministry through Instagram while Tom controls the website and does God's work through there. This way, Tom avoids falling into temptation and stays on the course that God has set out for him.

No matter how seemingly small, in-significant, or foolish it may seem to those on the outside looking in, it is necessary. It is all a part of a multiple move strategy that Tom must use to defeat Satan with and resist Satan's attempts to not only cause Tom to fall into sexual sin, but also to bait him out of his position in Christ. Satan wants to lure Tom away from God so that he can destroy him, his gift of eternal life (if he should choose not to repent), and most of all, affect the future generations that will come after him. Satan ultimately wants to destroy Tom's soul and his legacy.

Chapter 7

The Distraction Strategy

Even though many people claim that they are of the Christian faith, there seems to be a small number of those who understand what it is that they say they stand for. Have you ever noticed this? There can be a room full of self-proclaimed Christians, but there may only be two who use the Bible as a reference for how they lead their lives and stand apart from the world. Why is this so?

This is because Satan has successfully managed to pervert the meaning of what it means to truly live for God. He has done this through religion, denominationalism, the secularization of how we serve God and by perverting our view of Jesus Christ. He has done this through worldly worship and the obser-

vance of ungodly holidays (these are tradi-
tional but not biblical). He even normalized
the doctrine of his kingdom through television shows, games, horoscopes, books, music,
and holidays.

Religion

Religion is one of the greatest traps
for believers. It is easy to believe that being
religious is equivalent to being saved. This,
however, is the furthest thing from the
truth. Religion is man-made and is a distraction from the true purpose of following God.
Religion deceives people into believing that
routine and self-righteousness are needed to
receive eternal life. But remember that it was
the religious officials who could not even recognize their own Savior. Religion is just a part
of one's lifestyle. But if you are a believer
and have a heart for God, and you walk by
faith, then living a life for Christ is not a part
of your lifestyle; it is your lifestyle. Your re-

lationship with Jesus Christ is what matters, not your religion.

Denominations

Denominations are the second major distraction for believers. This is simply because the focus can easily become based upon which denomination is the correct one. The truth is that division amongst the church was never Christ's intention. This is evident in the book of 2 Timothy when Paul discusses the church in the last days. However, we are here and what matters is not how you do your praise breaks nor whether your baptism took place in the Red Sea or your church home. Instead, what matters is whether you have received Jesus Christ as your Lord and Savior, and have been baptized in the Holy Spirit. John 3:16 is all you need to be saved. The next step is to get baptized in the Spirit and in water (John 3:5), and lastly, you must continue to seek God and study His Word consistently to build your relationship with Him. Do not be distracted by titles and denominations. Remember, the reason that Christ died was so that we could all receive salvation by grace. That is the gospel. That is it and that is all.

Social Distractions

Satan was very crafty with this one. He has managed to distract, trap, and deceive both believers and non-believers. Satan's doctrine has been greatly normalized socially. What was once considered perversion to the world is now acceptable. Witchcraft is now in a lot of television shows made for children. Horoscopes are read like the daily newspaper, and today's music is more satanically influenced than ever before. Sure, the music has a pleasurable beat, but what is being ministered through our ears and hearts is poison. God revealed to me why I was once a slave who'd fallen into this trap. I noticed that I never really had a tolerance for the language of foolishness. Therefore, when I thought about the lyrics of some of the songs that I loved, I was perplexed. I asked God why I was so in love with songs with such foolish nonsense or satanic speech that I otherwise would have rejected. God pointed out to me that it was because of how seductive and addictive the beat was. It is no coincidence that many rappers today give terrible interviews; when they talk, they could literally cause a person's ears to bleed because they lack wisdom. Not all, but a lot of them truly have nothing of value to offer when they speak. Yet, we listen to their music and consume their lyrics because of the catchy beats behind it. This subconsciously seduces us to agree with the spirit behind the music, even though we claim to not agree with it in the natural. Next thing we know, three years down the road, we are living by principles that we once said we would never live by. Furthermore, there are popular children's storybooks and games that encourage witchcraft and Satanism. Satan knows to attract children because they are more open and impressionable. However, we cannot blame them. We, as adults, are supposed to guide them, and if we have allowed them to fall into Satan's arms, then we can only point the finger at ourselves. Looking at the state of this new generation, I must say with great sadness that we have truly failed them. Therefore, we have to be aggressive with spreading God's Word and rebuking what is not of God, and we must do this while educating ourselves and our youth about what actually is of God and what is not.

Holidays

This section will focus on major holidays that Satan has used to distract believers and non-believers through perversion and desensitization. According to History.com, Christmas, Easter, and Halloween are all holidays that originally stemmed from pagan beliefs and rituals. Though some of these claims and some information about the roots of these holidays are controversial, it is still worth looking into to make certain that we are not partaking in anything that offends God. Halloween stems from a pagan Celtic tradition. This observance took place on October 31st, and was known as Samhain (pronounced saw-win). Samhain was a time to observe the end of summer and the beginning of harvest. The Celtic Priests, the Druids, would predict the future and would build bonfires for the Celts to burn their crops and make animal sacrifices to their gods. They also believed that the line between the world of the living and the world of the dead would become thin around this time. It was also very possible, in their minds, that evil spirits, as well as their loved ones, could return and enter this world. They also believed that the living could end up in the world of the dead if they were not careful. They would wear costumes to ward off evil spirits that they believed could cross over from the spirit world; they did this to avoid having those spirits recognize them.

Another observance incorporated into the Allhallowtide was the Pantheon, which was declared a day of honoring Christian Martyrs who had passed; this holiday took established on May 13th by Pope Boniface in 609 A.D. But it was then moved to November 1st by Pope Gregory III. This became known as All Saints Day. November 2nd would then become known as All Soul's Day to honor the dead. In England, children would go from door to door for All Soul's Day as an act of service or charity for their churches, and they would offer to pray for the people's dead relatives in exchange for a soul cake, food, or money. These children would stand on the graves of their loved ones, eat their soul cakes and pray for the dead. While this is not the complete origin of trick or treating, this is one of the early practices. While it is understood in some Christian beliefs, such as in the Roman Catholic church, that we can pray for the dead, some scriptures speak against this act. Therefore, we should not be participating in these rituals. There are some scriptures that are said to support the concept of souls being trapped in purgatory and needing prayer. In other words, they are told to support the concept of praying for the dead.

The concept of purgatory is found in the apocryphal book of 2 Maccabees 12:41-45 (NRSV). When Judas Maccabeus collects money from the family members of their loved ones who have passed and prays for their souls so that they may have their sins blotted out, this is one of the references made for purgatory. But the only way that one's sin can be blotted out is through the grace given by Jesus Christ when we believe in Him and confess that He is our Lord and Savior, as stated in John 3:16. That is the only price that needs to be paid, and Jesus paid it on the cross. Luke 16:19-26 and Corinthians 3:11-15 are also referred to as evidence that purgatory exists.

Luke 16:19-26 NIV

"There was a rich man who was dressed in purple and fine linen and lived in luxury every day. At his gate was laid a beggar named Lazarus, covered with sores and longing to eat what fell from the rich man's table. Even the dogs came and licked his sores. The time came when the beggar died and the angels carried him to Abraham's side. The rich man also died and was buried. In Hades, where he was in torment, he looked up and saw Abraham far away, with Lazarus by his side. So he called to him, 'Father Abraham, have pity on me and send Lazarus to dip the tip of his finger in water and cool my tongue, because I am in agony in this fire.' But Abraham replied, 'Son, remember that in your lifetime you received your good things, while Lazarus received bad things, but now he is comforted here and you are in agony. And besides all this, between us and you a great chasm has been set in place, so that those who want to

go from here to you cannot, nor can anyone
cross over from there to us.'"

This story is in reference to Hades, not purgatory. Also, as stated in this scripture, the
fixed chasm mentioned prevents souls from
getting out.

Corinthians 3:11-15 NIV

"For no one can lay any foundation other than
the one already laid, which is Jesus Christ. If
anyone builds on this foundation using gold,
silver, costly stones, wood, hay or straw,
their work will be shown for what it is, because the Day will bring it to light. It will be
revealed with fire, and the fire will test the
quality of each person's work. If what has
been built survives, the builder will receive a
reward. If it is burned up, the builder will suffer loss but yet will be saved—even though
only as one escaping through the flames."

When reading these verses, one may
believe that Paul is speaking of a literal fire.

However, the fire is symbolic of God's judgment. Our foundation must be Jesus Christ, and our motives must be driven by Jesus Christ. The church and whatever else we build in this life should be built and based on Jesus Christ. Christ is the foundation that can pass the test of fire or God's judgment. Anything else will burn in the lake of fire.

Deuteronomy 18:9-11 NIV also contradicts the concept of purgatory, along with the practices and rituals that take place during these holidays. We are not, as God's children, to practice what other nations practice. We are not to turn to witchcraft, sorcery, or attempt to communicate with the dead. What is now known as Halloween and the Day of the Dead (El Dia De Los Muertos), where families will sometimes leave food out for their ancestors, were rooted in the very practices that our Father forbids. Some of these rituals, especially during the Day of the Dead or All Souls Day, are still practiced by some believers today.

But according to scripture, this is offensive to God.

Christmas is another holiday that stems from a pagan ritual that took place on December 21st; it is called the Winter Solstice and it is disguised as a celebration of new life. The original name of this day was Yule, which the Norse celebrated in Scandinavia. Many of us have heard the line "Yuletide carol." This is the tradition that is being referred to in that song. Another day that influenced what is to-day known as Christmas is Saturnalia. According to history.com, the Romans would celebrate Saturn, the god of agriculture, by having the order in their empire switched. For example, slaves would get to be slave masters and vice versa for one month. On December 25th, members of the middle class in Rome would celebrate their "god of the unconquerable sun," Mirtha's, birthday. In their belief system, this was regarded as a sacred holiday. There was speculation from the Puritans that Pope Julius I decided to use December 25th to recognize the birth of Jesus Christ to "purify" this holiday and "cleanse" it of its pagan roots. It is not even certainly known whether Jesus was born on December 25th or any time in winter, for that matter. Santa Claus, which falls more in line with the secularization of this holiday, was created after St. Nicolas, a monk who gave away all his inherited wealth, helping those in need. He also became known as the protector of children and sailors. But another interesting fact is that Santa Claus has many similarities with Oden (also spelled Odin), another pagan god that the Germans believed in and feared during their mid-winter holiday; they both had animal guides and made trips in the sky during the night. The only difference is that Santa Claus would make these trips to see if he would grant gifts to those who were "nice" and not those who were "naughty," while Oden was looking to see who would obtain prosperity and who would receive death. They even both have long white beards. For any believer that celebrates this day, especially with the inclusion of Santa Claus, be careful as you may be:

1. Exalting a historical figure over God.
2. Unintentionally giving reverence to a pagan deity.

Odin/Santa Claus

Lastly, Easter is another holiday that is said to stem from pagan traditions. This is mainly due to the concept of the Easter egg, which was said to represent fertility in a pagan culture. It is even said that the word Easter comes from Eostre, who is the goddess of fertility in Anglo-Saxon culture. This claim was made by St. Bede the Venerable in his book, *Historia Ecclesiastica Gentis Anglorum* or *Ecclesiastical History of the English People.* Other historians claim that word derives from the Old High German vocabulary word, eostarum, which means new life and new beginnings. While there are disagreements amongst historians regarding the roots of these holidays, particularly Easter, it is worth considering that the celebration of these holidays is not found in scripture. We must be mindful of what it is that we are celebrating and subscribing to.

Satan is using holidays as a distraction as well. How? He has found ways to sneak the practices that exalt him and his doctrine through idol worship and pagan practices. He distracts us by making it more festive and making it appear to be an opportunity for family gatherings. He appeals to big corporations with greed to push these holidays and generate a large amount of money. Satan and his kingdom are desperate to pull believers away from God and will find countless creative and underhanded ways to distract us, take our eyes off scripture, and desensitize us to abominations and abominable practices by normalizing them through media marketing and promotion.

The purpose of including this information is not to scrutinize anyone who observes these holidays. However, for believers, Jesus' resurrection should be recognized and celebrated every day, along with the observance of the birth of our Christ. This also includes days of worship. God is amazing every day, so He is worthy of being worshiped every day.

This is why we should not follow pagan practices or rituals, nor should we even acknowledge false gods or any characters who resemble or represent these false gods. God has spoken against these practices, and even though everything and everyone who has accepted Jesus as their Lord and Savior is covered in His blood, we are to honor our relationship with Him. If we have a relationship with our God and love our God, then we should be careful not to partake in activities that offend Him, even if the rest of the world is doing it. We are to be set apart from the world and not be of this world. This is not to encourage believers to be legalistic, but to encourage believers to be prudent. We must recognize where certain trends and traditions stem from and not just blindly follow them. These practices stem from pagan idol worship.

Money, Money, Money, Money

Another great example of the world blatantly disrespecting God through idol worship is the bull on Wall Street of New York City representing the stock market. While I do not know of anyone making animal sacrifices to this bull, Americans sacrifice their lives to obtain what many of the citizens in this country worship the most: money. Satan has used currency to distract the entire population from what matters: our salvation and relationship with God. People rejoice when there is a "bullish" stock market and nearly lose their minds when there is a bear market. That is worship. It is ironic how God was angered by the calf Aaron built in Exodus 32:2-5 for the Israelites, and today, the same idol has been made. Only this time, it is even bigger and is the male adult version of the first idol that God's chosen people had created. Or maybe it isn't irony, but man's act of arrogance.

The "Charging Bull"

As believers, we must separate ourselves from this behavior and refrain from
committing these abominable acts of the
world. If they do not stem from scripture, we
must be very careful when accepting these
practices. We must know what we are coming
into agreement with. We must not tolerate

anything that would cause us to compromise our faith or our relationship with our Father in Heaven.

Chapter 8

The Spirit of Bondage Play

Whether or not society would like to admit it, being in bondage has been normalized. One would be considered odd in today's culture if that person were not bound by something. Those who have committed to changing their lives and have refrained from participating in certain activities understand this well. They have received the famous "You don't (fill in the blank)?" question.

- "You don't drink?"
- "You don't smoke?"
- "You don't curse?"
- "You don't have sex?"

They then give you this confused look, and your spirit can tell that they have automatically labeled you 'the outcast' in their minds.

But what many don't understand is that what they are asking is, "Why aren't you bound like we are bound?" or "How do you have the nerve to be free?"

Think about a celebrity who fell into the life of drug addiction. Unfortunately, there are countless of them who can be named. But, when you hear their stories, you typically hear that they did not enter the industry with this issue. While some may argue that this was always an issue for those individuals even before they entered the industry or a relationship, the fact remains that they were introduced to it somehow. The only things that were there before they were bound were their flesh, their desires, their curiosity (which was explained in chapter 5 with Adam and Eve), and the seed that the enemy planted through some medium.

When I was in nursing school and doing my clinical rotation in the NICU step down, I saw an underweight baby who was addicted to crack because her mother was a slave to this addiction while pregnant with her. Satan attacked this child very early and used her mother as the pawn. Because her mother was not set free from her addiction, she could not be with her child, nor could she nurse her. The little girl had to rely on the nurses in the NICU to take care of her.

Satan attacked that young child in the game early. This was his way of making the first move, using the Tennison gambit, by sacrificing his pawn, the mother, to get to the child. This was similar to when Satan used Pharaoh as a pawn to kill all the male newborns to get to Moses (Exodus 1:15–22). Or when he used King Herod to try to get to Jesus (Matthew 2:16). To go a step further, this is similar to when Satan uses adults, bound by the spirit of perversion, to harm children sexually or physically. Unfortunately, it is typical for these children to grow up confused, hurt, and spiritually open to being used as Satan's pawns as well. They may willingly become his pawns because, in their souls, someone needs to feel the pain that they are feeling. As a result, the poison is passed down from generation to generation, and they are all bound by whatever familiar spirit that has been preying on their families, communities, or regions. Therefore, it is imperative that all of us get healing from our past hurts and traumas so that we are not susceptible to being used as Satan's pawns to hurt others.

Another way that Satan uses people as pawns is when he uses our friends to lead us into bondage. Due to past experiences, I do not engage in drinking, not just because I am a Christian, but because I no longer have the desire to. I can recall an incident I had while celebrating my 25th birthday. A few of my friends made it their duty to get me drunk, and after declining multiple times, I gave in to peer pressure and drank liquor. I became intoxicated and I purchased a plane ticket to Los Angeles that night. The next morning, I had a headache and was vomiting. I shared my experience with a friend the next day, and she laughed at me. She also told me that I am not a drinker.

I did not enjoy the feelings I experienced while regaining my sobriety. I felt disoriented, I had headaches and after eating and drinking, I felt nauseous. I later found out that the young woman who was supposed to be my friend at the time did not have my best interest at heart. This was evident when we went to Los Angeles, which is another story for another time. Whether she knew it or not, Satan was using her as a pawn to lead me into a life of drugs, alcohol, and partying. His goal was to get me bound to that spirit. However, that just was not my cross to bear. I had other issues that I was battling, such as maladaptive daydreaming and pornography that I had been in bondage to for years.

Another common way that Satan uses people as pawns is through romantic relationships. There are so many toxic relationships that are keeping individuals bound. Should the relationship end without them experiencing deliverance, they would then subconsciously search for that familiar spirit in another individual. These spirits can be sexual sin, drug and alcohol abuse, physical abuse, emotional abuse, codependency, and self-sabotage.

Another angle Satan takes is through the media. There are so many songs, movies, television shows, and commercials that promote the behaviors that God speaks against. God's intention for these boundaries is not to keep us bound, but to keep us free. God sets boundaries because He loves us. Satan sets traps because he hates us.

The pawn in this play is the people who plant these negative seeds. Now, these can be non-believers as well as believers. Some believers may still be young in the faith or they have not fully let their worldly habits go. Other believers may genuinely feel that something is harmless and just simply need to be corrected. Then, there are the "believers" who are not believers but claim to be followers of Jesus; they are not really dedicated to the faith, or worse, are only wearing the guise of a believer to bait other believers.

The knights are the demonic spirits such as addiction, fantasy, or any self-sabotaging behavior. The rooks are the principalities which, in this case, is bondage.

The Counter Strategy

Stay in your position and allow God to be the player and the strategist. Do not try to take His place by hanging out or getting in a relationship with someone who is not of God and say that you are "witnessing" to that person. You can be the light in someone's life, but it is not your job to be the guardians of their faith, though some believers think that they can do this with non-believers who are their friends, family members, or significant others. If the person who played the role of Satan's pawn was a parent or another adult who hurt you when you were in your vulnerable state, or if you were completely blindsided, do not blame yourself. Do not walk in unforgiveness against any of these individuals, and do not be unforgiving towards yourself. Remember which piece you are. You are the queen, God's most valuable piece in the game, second to the king. So, move accordingly. Pray to God to expose the spirit that the individual is bound by and the spirit that is keeping you bound. What usually happens when you do this is you get set free because the spirit is exposed. I had a dream that I had an infection that seemed random and resulted in me having black spots all over my body. I was scared because I thought that I would be alienated by people who would not want to be infected with whatever I had. I went to someone I felt I could trust and could help me, and as I rolled up my sleeves to show her the spots, they were gone. Perplexed by this dream after waking up, I asked God what the dream was about. He did not reveal the answer to me right away, but later that day when I was worshiping Him, God revealed the meaning to me. He said that once I exposed my blemishes, which were the ungodly spirits I was bound by, I would be free from them, and the "infection" would be cured. Ladies and gentlemen who are reading this, expose those spirits or ask God to expose them to you if you cannot recognize them so that you can be set free! If you are not instantly set free, pray to get set free. Chances are, you are not yet free because you are still in love with your slave master. Once you are free, you will then have the capacity to pray for others to get set free. This may cause them to get set free because you are interceding for them if their hearts are not hardened. They can then become pieces that God has gained. Satan hates this, but as the church, we have this kind of power. Instead of submitting to these satanic attacks, we can lead these people to Christ, and He can set Satan's pawns free and bring them to His side of the board.

Chapter 9

The Mirroring Strategy

In chess, some opponents use a strategy called mirroring, also known as copycat chess. This is when the opposing side, typically black, copies the moves of his or her opponent. Those who are adept at this game consider this to be a terrible strategy. It makes the opponent predictable and is more of a tactic as opposed to a strategy. Satan does this as well. Though this is not his killer strategy, it is the most deceitful when dealing with Satan's kingdom.

This method rarely works in favor of the copycat. An example of this would be in the book of Exodus 7:22. When Moses was showing the works and miracles of Yahweh (our God), Pharaoh and his servants copied these works to avoid having their idols be discredited. But Pharaoh's copycat methods did not work in his favor and eventually led him to his demise.

The original will always beat the copycat. This is simply because the original already starts at least one step ahead of the copier. Therefore, mirroring your opponent is not advised in chess because you are automatically at a disadvantage. You will always be at least one step behind. This has been shown to us in the Bible as well as in history. Even when the copycats seem to be prospering more than the original, their victories are short-lived, and they are at a loss when they are unable to recalibrate and rebound. Meanwhile, the original has already moved on to the next step. It is one thing to be inspired by someone but still go your own route, adding your own little spin on that individual's methods, but to be a complete copycat makes you a phony, and you will always be on the losing end.

As believers, we understand that Satan does, in fact, mirror God a lot. But we can also still be deceived. Therefore, we must remain in God's Word and ask Him to expose to us the areas where we are weak. As mentioned before, Satan studies us until he knows where we fall short. He is desperate to capture people from God's church. He will mirror God but will also appeal to us by playing on our weaknesses. As mentioned before, many people are weak in sexual sin nowadays, even those who are following God. Understanding this, Satan has influenced and deceived some pastors or even his pawns who pose as "pastors." These men and women claim to serve God, but they preach a false gospel. Satan has caused them to build churches and declare that fornication is "old news" and no longer applies to today's time. Believers who do not address this weakness of theirs or refuse to use their Christ-given authority to have dominion over the spirit of fornication are baited into these ungodly churches. But that is not all. Some believers simply will not get into God's Word; they would rather follow a man than obey God. Therefore, they are easily deceived. They are no different from the people who followed Pharaoh in the book of Exodus. They all followed him to the grave.

Satan will never win with this tactic, and he knows this. That is not where the issue lies. The point of the mirroring method is to deceive God's people or people who would have potentially followed God. There are many ways that Satan has mirrored God in the past, and still mirrors God to this very day. This is all in hopes of tripping some faithful servants or potentially faithful servants as they run the race.

False Prophets

In the book of 1 Kings, Jezebel was a queen who worshiped Baal, and she had false prophets who followed her. They were mirroring God's true prophet, Elijah. When reading 1 Kings, one can notice that Elijah, while upset at the disobedience of Ahab's rebellion against Yahweh, did not need to go out of his way to prove that he was a true prophet. He was confident that God's Word would come to pass.

When Ahab asked Naboth for his vineyard, Naboth refused. Saddened by this, Ahab sulked and refused to eat. His wife, Jezebel, was disturbed by his vexation. Once she learned of the reason for Ahab's sadness, she stated that he would get the vineyard as if she were a prophetess. To force this prophecy into existence, she wrote letters in the king's name and had Naboth killed. Once Naboth was killed, Ahab took his vineyard. Elijah then received a word from the Lord and prophesied to Ahab in 1 Kings 21:23 NIV stating, "And of Jezebel the LORD also said, 'The dogs shall eat Jezebel within the walls of Jezreel.'" This happened, and Elijah did not have to manipulate any circumstances to force this prophecy to come to pass. Ahab, who had repented a few times before his end, had a hand in these ungodly acts that took place in his kingdom. But Jezebel is the focus of this section. Jezebel refused to repent; she protected her pride just as this principality does today. Therefore, she was eaten by dogs in 2 Kings 9:35-37. False prophets will never prosper while operating under the spirit of deception. Many of them know this in their hearts, while others have had their hearts hardened because they refuse to repent. So, their demise is what many would say is warranted. However, just as Ahab and other false prophets followed Jezebel, those who follow them typically have a similar fate. Therefore, it matters who you receive a word from. Stay in prayer and pray about every word and prophecy that you are given. Test the spirits, as stated in 1 John 4:1-3 ESV, so that you are not led astray.

Jezebel

Understand that for Jezebel, a Phoenician, to have rule over the nation of Israel, Ahab, an Israelite, had to intermarry with a pagan nation. In other words, one of God's very own stepped out of position against God's order and took Satan's bait. The pawn, in this instance, was Jezebel herself. But bear in mind that the spirit that was in Jezebel existed long before the day of her birth. It is only because she allowed this spirit to do a number on her and possess her until it drove her to her death, unlike any other man or woman who had operated under the influence of this spirit. This is why we classify this spirit as the Jezebel spirit or principality today. But what made Ahab allow Satan's pawn, Jezebel, to enter the kingdom of Israel? The spirit of fear.

Because Ahab submitted to the spirit of fear, which is the knight in this play, it was easy for Jezebel to infiltrate his territory. The Jezebel principality is the rook. Leviathan or the spirit of pride, is the queen. This is how the king of the opposing side, Ahab, was captured as a result. This move that Satan made when using the Jezebel principality in this play was so dynamic in history that Ahab himself is now a spirit that is a part of the Jezebel principality's lineup. The Ahab spirit comes in when someone in authority, like Adam in Genesis, relinquishes his or her power to someone who was intended to be under his or her rule. This act is typically driven by fear and a lack of faith in God. Ahab desperately needs a Jezebel because of his fear of walking in authority. He wants the title and the position but not the responsibility. Therefore, only a back-leading subordinate that lusts after the kind of power that their superior has will fulfill this task. Hence, they will allow themselves to be seduced by the

Jezebel spirit and take rule over Ahab. This is a prime example of Satan taking one of God's pieces. This was only allowed to happen because Ahab stepped out of position and took control of the game. Therefore, God removed his hand from the board. Ultimately, Satan's doctrine spread throughout the nations and affected Ahab's generation and the ones that followed.

Ahab sat on the wrong side of the board when he did not allow God to be the player in the game. How many times have you disallowed God to be the player of the chess game in your life? Or are you still under the impression that your life is not the equivalent of a chess game as well? Ahab did not realize that he was in a game of chess. Worst of all, he had not the slightest clue as to who his true opponent was. Lastly, he was playing the wrong game. Ahab's only goal was to say, "King me," and Satan's goal was to say, "Checkmate!" These are two different games.

One phrase indicates that one has an advantage but not always a win. The other phrase is only stated when there is a definite win.

False Doctrine

False doctrine is just that—false. This is when Satan takes God's doctrine and perverts it. He typically does this by using people who want to pollute the Word to fulfill their own selfish desires (1 Timothy 6:3-5). They spread this false teaching and manage to lead thousands and even hundreds of thousands astray, forming what many know as cults. But why would they not solely live the way they want to live and leave others out of it? Well, the first reason is power. Leaders of cults have a thirst for power. Secondly, they need people to validate them. When one stands on God's Word and His principles, they do not need the validation of others. Jesus was able to stand alone, for example. He only asked people to follow Him to show that He could help them see the light and be the light in their lives. People also willingly followed Him without Him even asking because He walked in confidence and truth. Thirdly, misery loves company. Whenever you look deeper into these occult followings, you learn that they are not genuinely happy, and a lot of times, these false systems and doctrines are built on their hurt and trauma, such as cults that speak ill of other races and tell the lie that Jesus is only for them. Even in the cults that are not based on trauma but are based solely on desire, like the desire for polygamy or riches, the people that follow these false teachings are still miserable. The previous two desires mentioned, polygamy and riches, are birthed from greed, one of the seven deadly sins, and greed is never satisfied. This is the same for every follower and leader of these cults; they are miserable because they are never satisfied. Only God can satisfy our souls and quench our thirst (Isaiah 55:1, John 7:37).

Counterfeit Religion and Belief Systems (Astrology, Witchcraft, and New Age Teachings)

There is nothing new under the sun (Ecclesiastes 1:9). God has already done and proven what the world tries to do, discover, or prove today. Satan mirrors a lot of God's moves as a way of bargaining with us. If we do it Satan's way, we can have the blessings without the accountability, or so it would appear. However, nothing is free, and you will always have to pay the price no matter what belief is that you choose to adhere to. Both God and Satan want you to pay with your life. The difference is, God wants your life so He can improve it and grant you eternal life, but Satan wants your life so he can destroy it and lead you to eternal damnation.

Unfortunately, many people accept Satan's bargain and take a counterfeit over what is authentic. These counterfeit belief systems include New Age teachings, Astrology, and the Law of Attraction. So, why would people accept counterfeits? Well, it is more convenient. You will never have to work as hard as you would for real money when working for counterfeit money. The only work that you would have to do is printing if you were to only create counterfeit cash. If you become truly skilled at creating counterfeit money, the work would get easier. But learning a new skill and then trading your time for an income, even if you eventually obtain passive income, takes a great deal of hard work. No one who is financially successful was able to get a free ride to success. Many understand this concept regarding money, but do not make the same connection concerning their faith. The bottom line is that the counterfeit always comes at what seems to be a cheaper price but is more costly. Note that counterfeiting money or the use of counterfeit money is a federal crime. We will all have to give an account for what we have done on this Earth, including who we chose to follow

and serve, whether we accept that reality or
not. The problem is that many people do not
see it as a big deal. They believe that you can
serve who or what you want to serve and that
there will be no consequences for rejecting
the one and only Creator. This is what the
entire New Age system is built on. But in this
section, we will see just how much of a counterfeit this system is.

A lot of New Age thinkers accept astrology as a guide for their lives. There is an
ongoing debate amongst believers about
whether astrology is okay for us to follow. I
once found that there was a lot of truth in it
when I used to follow it, but one thing is for
certain; anything that is exalted higher than
God must be cast down. God is the Creator of
the stars and the universe. Therefore, the
creation must not be placed above the Creator. I renounced astrology after receiving
more knowledge about it, as I now understand
that it is demonic and should not be followed

by believers of Yahushua. Here is a comparison chart showing the similarities between the New Age belief system and God's Word and plan.

God's Moves	Satan's Moves
Yahweh	The Universe
Faith	The Law of Attraction
Prayer	Meditation
God-Ordained Relationship	Twin Flame
Prophets	Fortune Tellers
Prophecy	Fortune Telling
Deliverance Ministers	Witches/Warlocks
The End Times	The Age of Aquarius
God's Will	Destiny
God's Purpose	Chiron
The Flesh	Lilith
Soul Ties	Cords
The Holy Spirit	Conscience
Guardian Angels	Spirit Guides

Yahweh vs. The Universe: Who is the Real Creator?

Believers say that Yahweh is the Creator, and followers of the New Age movement say that the universe is the creator. Personally, I find it very hard to believe that the universe can inspire writings and documents that can stand the test of time. Believers see the universe as inanimate. However, non-believers see God or Yahweh as nonexistent. Some believers of the New Age teaching, especially those who accept astrology, believe that there is a God, but they think that God does not have a specific name or form. Therefore, God can be the universe, the grass, the trees, water, or anything that one can feel inspired by. But is it creation that we are inspired by or is it the fact that they were created in the first place that inspires us? If we analyze the world and the people around us, we can see that everything is connected. We, as people, can create. When we create these items, we, as the creators, get the credit. The creation does not get the credit. Therefore, the verse where God states that He will create man in His image (Genesis 1:26) is evidence that who we are and what we do is reflective of not just a higher power but a higher being. We are moral beings, and this does not come from nowhere. The higher power that we serve would most likely be a spiritual and moral being. The universe does not have morality and does not hold us accountable. However, Yahweh does. We are very big on rules and accountability, whether we want to honor this fact or not. The evidence of this is the laws that we have in place. It helps to maintain order, which prevents chaos, and preventing chaos ultimately prevents destruction. When we study Yahweh, we see that He too is about order and accountability. These are ways that we reflect the likeness of Him.

Faith vs. the Law of Attraction

Many may say that these are the same. The law of attraction utilizes the power of one's thoughts to manifest what it is that one would want in his or her life. If people are not careful, they can even bring their negative thoughts into manifestation. "It is the Law of Attraction which uses the power of the mind to translate whatever is in our thoughts and materialize them into reality," reports thelawofattraction.com. Faith also deals with thoughts. If you believe something, whether good or bad, it will likely come to fruition. "For as he thinks in his heart, so is he" (Proverbs 23:7, NKJV). So once again, faith and the Law of Attraction are similar. However, there is a key difference. The Law of Attraction gives credit to us and what we can do with our minds. When it comes to the Law of Attraction, we are overseeing and shaping our own destinies. It is easy to believe in this because it makes us feel powerful, and we are powerful to an extent. But where the source of our power comes from is the most important factor in all of this. Humans are flawed, and the mind is Satan's playground. Faith is a biblical concept, and it is believing in what we cannot see and Who we cannot see: Yahweh. It also has boundaries because it must be within God's will for it to come to pass. So, according to the Law of Attraction, if you want it, you can get it. But according to God, if you want it, you can get it if it is within God's will. Therefore, we are instructed not to pray amiss (James 4:3).

Prayer vs. Meditation

Prayer and meditation are used in similar ways and are even used interchangeably by some. I have heard on more than one occasion that prayer is a form of meditation. Though there is some truth to this, there is still something distinct about prayer. General meditation is used so that one can gain clarity and become centered with oneself. Prayer is also used to gain clarity, but it is not about becoming centered with oneself. Instead, it is about becoming intimate with the Lord. I have done meditations in the past. I have also prayed and continue to pray till this very day. Both have made me feel very present in the moment and have helped me to gain a lot of clarity. But I felt closer to God and more in alignment with my purpose through prayer. I gain more revelation through prayer and reached a higher level spiritually. Meditation is to achieve a higher level spiritually as well or, according to New Age terminology, a higher vibration, but it lacks intimacy. Intimacy strengthens relationships. Now, for the believers of Christ who wonder if it matters whether we pray or meditate, it does. God wants you to strengthen your relationship with Him, and that is done through prayer because it is communication with God through conversation. You cannot achieve this through meditation unless you are mediating on His Word and His Word alone.

God-Ordained Relationship Vs. Twin Flame Relationship

According to astrology and New Age teachings, a twin flame is not guaranteed to be in a relationship with you. However, according to their doctrine, if a person does meet his or her twin flame, the two of them will fulfill a divine purpose together. They both have attributes and qualities within each other that help them to grow, unlock their greatest potential, and they may even be pushed to confront some wounds that they may not have realized were inside of them. It is as if they are looking in the mirror. They also believe that not everyone meets or even marries their twin flame. But those who do are truly blessed and fulfilled, according to various astrology and New Age teachings. When this union happens, it demonstrates to other people what a divine connection between two people looks like. The twin flame connection is almost identical to a God-ordained relationship, mainly a God-ordained marriage. Not everyone will meet their God-ordained spouse. This can be for many reasons: impatience, lack of growth, or not following God wholeheartedly. Just like the twin flame, you are not to stress over whether you will meet or have already met your God-ordained spouse. You will know by the connection that you have and by the mere fact that your foundational beliefs are the same. All the same, another form of evidence is that your purpose is in alignment with one other's. A God-ordained marriage will enable both spouses to fulfill God's divine purpose for their lives, which is impacting the world. Ultimately, this type of relationship will minister to those who observe it and see its beauty and wholeness. As a result, God will be glorified. Proponents of both twin flame relationships and God-ordained relationships believe that lovers can't be attached to their partners. In other words, they must be willing to let go of that individuals to have them. God would not want you to idolize your wife or husband. According to both doctrines, if lovers are overly attached to their partners or pedestalize them, chances are, they will lose sight of their purpose.

The differences between these two relationships are that twin flames do not have to be married to fulfill their purpose. But God does want you to be married to your God-ordained spouse because marriage is a part of that divine ministry and purpose that God has for this relationship. Marriage reflects the relationship between Jesus and His bride: the church. Therefore, it is so important to God. A twin flame connection is believed to be reincarnated throughout several lifetimes. A God-ordained spouse or marriage only lives through one lifetime. The second difference mainly exists because of the difference in the two belief systems regarding whether reincarnation exists. Lastly, the twin flame relationship has a concept of "the runner." The runner is believed to be someone who may leave the relationship several times because of the intensity of the relationship. The runner can be either a man or a woman. However, in a God-ordained relationship, there rarely is a runner, and if there is, it is typically the woman because the man is the one who pursues. The Bible specifically stated that "He who finds a wife finds a good thing and obtains favor from the Lord" (Proverbs 18:22 NKJV). The woman pursuing the man and the man being "the runner" would be out of order for God. However, this concept, once again, is rare in a God-ordained marriage because both parties are typically spiritually mature enough in their walks with Christ by the time they meet; this allows them to handle the intensity that may come with a God-ordained relationship.

Prophets Vs. Fortune-Tellers

A prophet is anointed by God. If they are not anointed by God, then they are false prophets. An anointed prophet serves as a vessel or a medium for God. This way, through them, God can speak to His children. Though God already speaks to His children through the Bible generally, a prophet can be used by God to speak to a specific person, community, tribe, church, or generation. A prophet is typically sent by God, instead of people voluntarily going to them to receive a word, though this does happen. A prophecy comes to pass regardless of whether the prophecy is received.

A fortune-teller is a medium for Satan. A fortune teller takes part in witchcraft and will proudly call themselves a witch a lot of the time. They are literally telling people who they are. But because witchcraft has been demonstrated as a farce in Hollywood, many people tend not to take it seriously. This goes for both non-believers and believers. This is how Satan deceives the world by selling the lie that spiritual mediums and spiritual war-fare are merely fairy tales. But the spirit world is very real. Fortune tellers have clair-voyance. I even believe that some fortune tellers would have been God's prophets if Satan had not snatched them up. I believe this because some of them genuinely have the gift; it has just been perverted. But Satan only knows what God allows him to know. Satan would then give that same information to a fortune teller or "psychic," but would often only tell them what he would want them to know. Therefore, by the time the information gets to the psychic or fortune teller, the information has been greatly reduced. Lastly, a fortune teller or a witch can only have power if you give it to them. This means that their readings or fortunes can only come to pass if they are received. This is called witchcraft. I recently fell into a terrible habit of viewing some tarot card readings for my zodiac sign on YouTube. I knew better, but the curiosity was burning me inside. Still, there is no justi-fiable excuse for my behavior. I would not completely watch the videos. I only watched one video in its entirety. What I did was called cross-watching for someone else's zodiac sign. I was trying to use this to see what this person may have been doing or if we were destined to be together because I had a serious crush on the guy. The Holy Spirit convicted me. So, I then settled for just reading the titles and reading the comments. I was still wrong in this act, however. I became impatient and felt as if God was not moving fast enough in my romantic life. Therefore, I turned to Satanic mediums. I am embarrassed to type this, but it needs to be called out and exposed. This is the only way to defeat the enemy, as he thrives in the dark. This was evidence that I had made an idol out of this person and relationships in general. Whenever you are willing to sin or go outside of the will of God for something or someone, be it a crush, lover, spouse, relative, or goal, you have made an idol out of that person or thing. I needed to repent, but it was an addiction.

Finally, I read a title, and it stated that I was going to be robbed. In the comment section of this reading, some people confirmed that they had been robbed. I shut my phone off and felt terrible. This laid heavily on my heart after I read that message. God, who had not left my side, though I was cheating on Him, asked me, "Do you receive it?" I told Him, "No." Later on that week, I thought I had been robbed as one of my accounts did not look the way I thought it should have. I thought to myself, "This is my fault. I should have never entertained those things!" But a calming spirit came over me (God's Spirit) and reminded me to use good ole common sense. He told me to run through the calculations again. I had simply miscalculated, and thankfully was not missing any money from my accounts. Furthermore, I had never had any encounter with a robber under any circumstances. Nonetheless, that was the last time I fooled around with those tarot card readings. I then renounced the spirits of witchcraft, obsession, and idolatry. I told this story to say that fortune-tellings and readings, unlike prophecies, can only come to pass if we receive them. They can only have power if you give them power. Prophecies have the power of God and will come to pass whether you receive them or not. I can guarantee you that those people who claimed that they were robbed in the comment section of that video were only robbed because they had received the word from the enemy, whose job is to steal, kill, and destroy.

If you are reading this and you agree with any witches at this very moment, repent and turn your heart back to God. Wait on Him and pursue deliverance.

Deliverance Ministers vs. Witches and Warlocks

Deliverance ministers are anointed warriors of God who have the God-given power to cast out demons that have either influenced an individual or are possessing an individual. A witch, on the other hand, helps those demons and dark spirits get into a person. In the previous section, I discussed that for a witch to prosper and have power over you, you must agree with them, and you must be open to receive what they are either saying or casting. The same thing happens regarding deliverance ministers. Though they have the God-given power and God-given authority to cast demonic spirits out, the individual who is either influenced or possessed by these spirits must want freedom from these spirits. Therefore, they need to be open to receiving deliverance. Therefore, before going through deliverance, it is advised that you fast to receive deliverance; that is, of course, once you wholeheartedly desire to fall out of agreement with the devil and his servants. When reading the gospels, you will see that Jesus only cast demonic spirits out when the person came to Him. Not once did He barge into anyone's house and say, "You need deliverance! Let me heal you!" He simply presented the option by walking in truth and ministering to the people. Jesus understood that not everyone wanted to heal and that if they were to receive deliverance (which, chances are, they wouldn't have because they were too in love with their demons), they would go and invite the demons back in. When Jesus healed the man who was unable to walk, He asked him if he wanted to be healed (John 5:2-6). The truth is, not everyone wants to be healed. Some people benefit from being sick, or so they think. They are too in love with the attention that they receive, the extra help that they receive, and in some cases, the disability checks that they receive. The truth about deliverance is it is true freedom, and with great freedom comes great responsibility. Yes, I am a Spiderman fan, and that statement was a variation of the famous saying from the comics.

The End Times or Last Days vs. the Age of Aquarius

The zodiac cycle mimics God's timeline. Aries is considered a fire sign. In some instances, the Aries personality is believed to be confrontational and, in some cases, if they were what astrologers would call a dark-sided Aries, belligerent and stubborn. The Aries period, according to the zodiac cycle, was from approximately 2200 BC-1 AD. When dating the activities of Samson in Judges, King Saul, and King David, according to the Bible timeline on Biblehub.com, it is said that Samson walked the earth circa 1075 century BC. Saul, the first king of Israel's reign began circa 1043 BC, and David's reign as king began circa 1003 BC. My reason for dating these events is that, as we read in the Old Testament, the nation of Israel and pagan nations were stubborn, hardhearted, and defiant, according to God (Ezekiel 3:7). There was also a lot of war and bloodshed during this time. Even the sacrifices that had to be made to God involved the slaughtering of an animal. This was the period of the Law, according to the Christian faith. This lines up with what astrologers say about this being the age of Aries.

Then, according to various sources, Jesus was said to walk the Earth from approximately 6 BC to 33 AD. This was around when the age of Pisces is said to have begun. More specifically, it is said that the age of Pisces began in the year 1 AD. Each zodiac cycle is said to be approximately 2000 years each. Some sources still say that the age of Pisces has not completely ended, while others say that it has. According to astrology, the Pisces' zodiac sign and the age is believed to be a time of spirituality. Is it a coincidence that this was when Jesus was giving spiritual teachings on the Earth, speaking against violence and preaching love instead? Whose crucifixion was the start of a new belief that required His followers to be more spiritual? Remember, in Acts 1:8, when Jesus appeared to

His disciples before ascending to Heaven, He stated that He would send a comforter: the Holy Spirit. This took place during the beginning age of what proponents believe to be the era of Pisces. We are now believed to be in the age of Aquarius, and some say that we are not quite in the age of Aquarius yet, but are approaching it. Whether we are close to entering or have already entered what some call the age of Aquarius, we are seeing people increasingly lean toward their understanding. Many people who subscribe to this belief state that we are in the "information age." Many people are renouncing teachings like those of Christianity because, according to them, they "know better." First, Adam and Eve ate from the Tree of the Knowledge of Good and Evil. Consequently, they became "enlightened" and "knew better" too; look at where that brought us. Secondly, this is a very prideful attitude that man has taken on. Man has now put himself on a pedestal and believes that he knows better than God. No, scratch that because, in his mind, God does not exist. Man now leans toward his own intellect and worships himself.

This is a sign of "the last days" or "the end times" before Jesus returns to earth (2 Timothy 3:2). The zodiac cycle mirrors and even proves God's Word, because it is Satan's attempt to disguise himself as God by taking Kingdom principles and adding a few lies to them here and there. Satan does not have an issue with us accepting what God says. He takes issue with us acknowledging God and worshiping God. The truth is that Satan wants us to worship anything but God because he is envious of God and jealous of us; this is because he knows how much God loves us. Never forget that Satan was cast out of Heaven (Isaiah 14:4-17) because he let his pride, envy, lust for power, and greed get the best of him. He knows what Heaven is like, and if he is desperately fighting to keep us away from it, it must truly be good.

147

God's Will vs. Destiny

In this section, by God's will, I am specifically referring to God's sovereign will. In other words, this is the type of will that is inevitable regardless of your actions. It is God's sovereign will to have Jesus' return. It was God's sovereign will to have Jesus die for our sins. It is true that we have free will, but God permits certain actions by us, while not allowing other actions. Nevertheless, our actions and decisions do not and cannot affect God's sovereign plan. When events happen in our lives, whether favorable or unfavorable, they are in accordance with God's will for our lives. A worldly or New Age way of thinking would refer to this as destiny. This may seem more attractive than God's will because there is a belief that you can take control of your destiny, especially when using the law of attraction. But God's will be God's, and we do not have the right nor the ability to take control of it. Therefore, we can ask amiss during prayer because it is outside of God's will.

Trying to control an outcome outside of God's will through the manipulation of people or forces on Earth is witchcraft, which is not of God but of Satan.

God's Purpose vs. Chiron

God's purpose for your life was set from the time that you were created. So, even before you were born, God had a plan for you. Often, you will find that God's purpose for your life would be revealed through your talents. For example, if you have been very skilled in music-making, typically, this would indicate that God's purpose is for you to minister to people through music. In New Age teaching, it is acknowledged that everyone has a purpose on this Earth, but in this type of teaching, and more specifically in astrology, it is believed that you could find this purpose in your natal chart. This section on your natal chart is known as Chiron. Chiron is the god of wound healing, according to Greek mythology. The irony was that Chiron could

heal others' wounds but was unable to heal
his own wounds. It is believed that the zodiac
sign where Chiron lies on one's natal chart
determines how a person will utilize his or her
gifts to heal others. However, it is God's will
for us to get healing through His Son, Christ
Jesus. Through our gifts, we minister to others and lead them to Christ to receive the
healing that they need. It was never intended
for us to take on a God-sized task and heal
others' wounds based on our strength and
talents alone.

The Flesh vs. Lilith

The flesh is our natural, human-like
side. A lot of times, it battles with our spirit.
During a fast, prayer, or worship, our flesh
causes us not to desire to do the very things
that the Spirit wants to do. Every day, a believer must fight with the flesh and the human heart, which God says is desperately
wicked (Jeremiah 17:9). There is another section of the natal chart that is called Lilith.

Lilith is said to be a woman in Jewish mythology who was rebellious and said to be Adam's first wife.

Lilith was believed to have been created at the same time Adam was created, and according to Jewish mythology, Lilith stood on the side of darkness. She and Adam would eventually split. Some sources say that she abandoned Adam, while others say that Adam divorced her because she wanted to have sex outside of the original intended position, which was with Adam on top of her. Instead, she wanted to be on top of Adam, but Adam refused.

Whether there is a correct sex position inside of marriage is another ongoing debate amongst believers. Some would argue that this act in the story is not ungodly, while others may argue that it is. But that is not the focus of this section. The purpose of discussing Lilith is to show the parallel between her and the flesh. Lilith, just like Chiron, is noted as a position on the natal chart in astrology. Lilith represents one's dark side. This is like the flesh because naturally, the flesh is perverse and desires many things outside of God's will. This is essentially the same thing that Lilith represents.

The Holy Spirit vs. the Human Conscience

The Holy Spirit was given to the believers of Jesus Christ on what is now known as the day of Pentecost. The Holy Spirit is simply God's Spirit living inside of us. He alerts us whenever something is out of order or off balance. He enlightens us, and if we are not careful, we could grieve His Spirit when we participate in ungodly activities. The Holy Spirit not only helps us to differentiate between holy and unholy behavior, but He also helps us stay on the holy path that God has set out for us. The equivalent of the Holy Spirit for New Age believers is the human conscience. It is believed to operate the same way as the Holy Spirit.

However, instead of showing us holy from unholy, it shows us right from wrong or good from bad. But what is right and what is good without God is subjective. What is considered right and good can vary from culture to culture. Now granted, we all have behaviors that are socially agreed upon as wrong, such as murder. But where do we get this from? Is this really from our minds and hearts when we naturally desire to do evil things? Many of us had passed on the opportunity of "knocking someone upside the head" when that person had seriously offended us during our states of immaturity. So yes, we all have moral consciousness, but wouldn't that indicate that there must be a creator of morality? New Age believers say that you can raise your consciousness through meditation and other practices such as walking through nature. This is like believers of Jesus strengthening their Holy Spirit through prayer and spending time in nature, which is a way for us to spend time with God, as well. The difference is that relying on human consciousness takes God out of the equation. It is, once again, a way to lean towards our intellect and understanding.

Soul Ties vs. Cords

Soul ties and cords are similar in principle. They just have different names and fall under various teachings. Soul ties and cords are spiritual bonds with other people that can be healthy or unhealthy. They can be formed through sexual encounters, conversations, intimate bonding, or any other encounter with an individual. You can have a soul tie with your friends, families, enemies, coworkers, and romantic partners. An example of a healthy soul tie or a God-ordained soul tie in the Bible is when David and Jonathan's friendship is described (1 Samuel 18:1). Soul ties can be cut through prayer and fasting.

Cords are believed to be cut through meditation and rituals. Both require studying about them and preparation before the cutting happens. The difference is that God breaks the soul tie, but New Age practitioners believe that they do the cord cutting themselves or even with someone guiding them through meditation or a cord-cutting ceremony. Once again, they are both similar to each other because they require the individual to be willing to let go of the individual they want to cut ties with spiritually. However, the difference is that cord cutting is a way that man takes matters into his own hands and does not allow God to handle the situation.

Guardian Angels vs. Spirit Guides

"For he will command his angels concerning you to guard you in all your ways" (Psalm 91:11 NIV).

God sends your guardian angels. Spirit guides are sent by Satan. When your guardian angels are trying to communicate with you,

you may see signs through events that take place in your life or even literal signs. When your spirit guide is trying to communicate with you, you will typically see numerical signs such as 333, 444, 1111, or 211. Each number represents a particular spirit guide.

There are light angels on the side of God, and there are dark angels on the side of Satan. Guardian angels send messages from God and ensure that we stay on God's path for us until we get to see Him in Heaven. Spirit guides send messages from Satan, the father of lies, and ensure that we stay on the path he has set for us, leading to hell. So, which one do you want to be in communication with?

The Wrap Up

The point of showing how all these beliefs reflect each other is to open the reader's eyes to expose the game that Satan is playing with the world. Anything that falls under New

Age teaching is not new. In many cases, it is a variation and a blatant copy of God's Word with a different name on it. It is a perversion of Yahweh's truth. This is how Satan deceives us. He has led many people astray by offering a counterfeit version of what God offers. The lie is that we can have God's promises without acknowledging God. We can take God's Word and either take the credit for it or even give the credit to Satan. Satan, in many of these cases, is being a copycat chess player.

Chapter 10

Let God Order Your Steps (Legal and Illegal Moves on the Board)

The last few chapters have shown what could happen in the middle game if we do not allow God to order our steps. It also shows how we can be in grave danger of falling victim to Satan's strategies by moving in our own will and not God's. If you are not on God's side, you are against Him, and if you are outside of His will, you are against Him. The only other team that you can be on is the side that Satan controls, whether voluntarily or involuntarily. This is because living outside of the will of God makes you more susceptible to Satan's attacks (and yes, even when he uses people, he is attacking them because he is leading them to destruction). Understand that we will always be attacked by Satan as much as God allows. This way, God can test our faith and strengthen it just as he did with Job. But when you step outside of God's covering, it is the equivalent of going into warfare with no shield.

As discussed in chapters 1 and 2, you will either be God's queen or Satan's pawn. There are only a certain number of movements each chess piece can make at a time. A pawn can only move forward one square except during three specific occasions: the first move, capturing, and en passant. On a pawn's first move, the player can move their pawn up to two spaces forward. When a piece is one space diagonally ahead of the pawn, the pawn can then capture the piece. A capture can also happen in en passant (French for in passing), which must be done immediately after a pawn from the opposing side moves two squares on the first move to a position that is adjacent to the pawn.

En Passant

A)

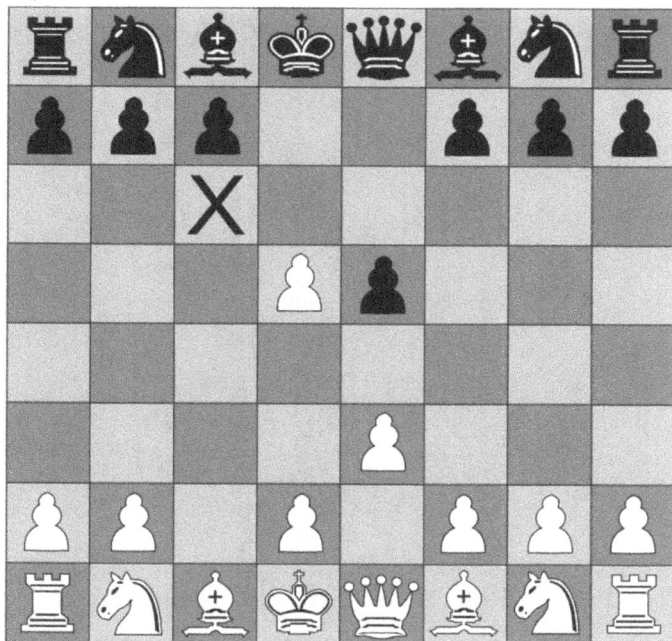

Black's pawn can either move one square or two squares on its first move. If black advances one square forward (where the box is highlighted), white's pawn would be

diagonally in front of it and able to capture it.

B)

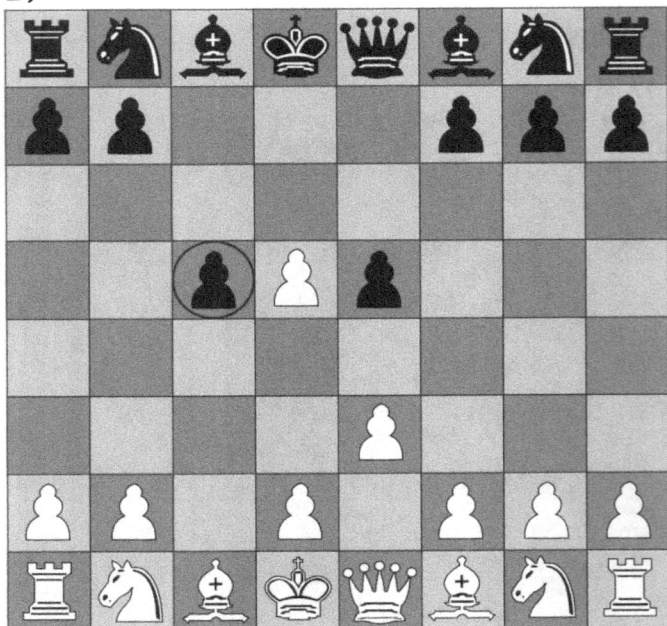

However, let's say that black's pawn advances two squares on its first move; it
will now be adjacent to white's pawn instead of diagonally in front of it.

C)

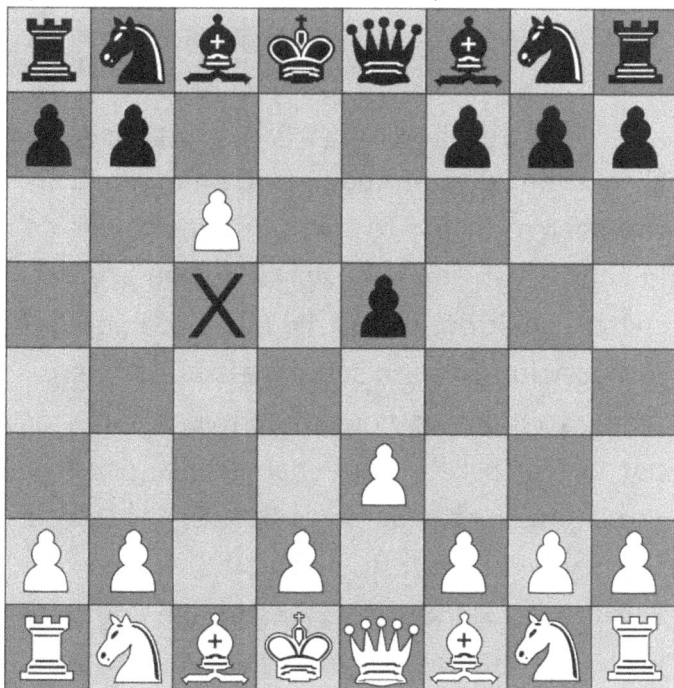

White can still capture black's pawn by advancing forward diagonally, which is only allowed in this move. This move can only be done in passing and must be done immediately. If white does not take this opportunity in the move, then white forfeits

**the opportunity to capture black's pawn in
passing.**

Satan will use his pawns, or people who
allow themselves to be used by him, to hurt
the people closest to them, just as pawns do
in chess. But this only works if they are in a
certain position. If God did not place you in
the position to be in someone's life or He is
trying to move you out of someone's life, do
not try to force God to change His mind by
remaining in that person's life. Otherwise, if
that individual is influenced by Satan and the
spirits that work for his kingdom in any way,
he or she can devour you. It would be the
equivalent of a capture. Typically, wise chess
players would not put their most valuable
pieces in such a position. For example, a
queen would not need to be in certain positions if a pawn or rook could be in that position. The queen should rarely be exposed to a
chance of being captured. Just imagine getting your queen swiped by a pawn. Unless you

have a strategy behind allowing that to happen, it would be a humiliating waste of a valuable piece.

Speaking of the queen, just how many steps can she make? Well, the queen can move an unlimited number of spaces in any direction on the board. But she and the pawn cannot jump ahead of any pieces that are in front of her. So, keep this in mind while remembering that when you are on God's side, you become a part of the church, which is God's queen piece. But do not try to jump ahead of those in front of you, as it is not legal in the game. The pieces in front of us are there to protect us. So, for example, if we try to jump ahead of our guardian angels, we are making an illegal move. Stepping outside of the boundaries that God has set for us can put us in grave danger. Anything or anyone in front of us who God is allowing to be there is there to protect us, directly or indirectly. This includes people from Satan's side. Some

people may say something or do something
with the ill intent of blocking us. But what
sometimes happens is that it indirectly pro-
tects us from greater harm. For example,
let's say you were applying for a job, but did
not get the job due to discrimination. Surely,
you are disappointed at first, but this leads
you to apply for other jobs. You have already
been protected from working in a toxic work
environment that focuses on superficial matters, instead of one's work ethic. But let's
take this a step further. Two weeks later, you
get a better and higher paying job. Two
months pass, and you then find out that the
job that rejected you has gotten shut down
due to OSHA violations. Had you received
that job, you would have had to look for another one within two months of being hired.
Sometimes, it's hard to see what we are being protected from when other pieces are in
our way. However, we must trust that God
knows what He is doing and that He under-

stands our value. Therefore, He will keep one of His most valuable pieces protected.

Just as the queen moves on the board, the church moves through evangelism, doing kind gestures and interceding for believers and non-believers through prayer. When we evangelize, we are spreading the Gospel. The Gospel is the living Word, and can spread like fire if taught correctly. The way to do this would be to use wisdom and witness to those who are willing to listen. If their hearts are hard, do not force them to believe and not argue. Move on Matthew 10:14. A kind gesture can reflect how our Christ demonstrates His love. This can be spread through word of mouth. Sometimes, we can bless someone so much that they just can't keep quiet about it. They are so overjoyed that they must tell someone about it. We also must be mindful that the same thing can happen with unkind gestures. Therefore, we must be careful not to intentionally offend someone because the word may get around, and as Christians, we do not want to misrepresent the God we serve. Sure, we can repent and get forgiveness, but we may have just caused someone who might have been open to giving Jesus a try to turn away from Him altogether. We must live our lives as if we are representatives of God, because we are. Lastly, interceding for people we know, people we know of, and even people that we don't know (this would typically happen when you are praying for an entire region) is a way to move around the world as a church. There is power in prayer, and there is power in intercessory prayer. If you do not have one already, you should keep a prayer list and continuously add to it. God hears our prayers, and we could stand in the gap for someone who may not be considering Him as an option. We, as the church, must know our power as the queen, and when we remain within the boundaries that God has set for us, we can do a lot of damage to Satan and his kingdom. We are a great threat to our opponent, and we should walk in confidence with this knowledge. We have the God-given authority to break down the enemy's kingdom through prayer and intercession, evangelism, and expressing love to others.

As mentioned before, the rooks, the knights, and the bishops are ranked higher than the pawns, but have the same job: to protect the king. They too have a specific way that they can move. Any movement outside of what they are allowed is illegal and out of order.

The Knight

The knight moves in an L shape on the board. This means that the knight can move two squares horizontally and then one square vertically. The knight can also move one square vertically, and then two squares horizontally. Both moves can be made in a forward or backward direction. The knight is also the only piece on the board that can jump over a piece that may be in front of it. Remember, God's knights are His angels, and Satan's knights are his demons. Both can only move in the directions that are allowed. Satan was once a knight for God. When he moved outside of the will of God, he made an illegal move. Consequently, he was cast out of Heaven along with the angels who followed him, who are now his servants. Angels protect us, and therefore, they can jump in front of us. Pride (the demonic queen) influences demons to jump in front of their pieces out of competition, not necessarily for protection. They only protect themselves and the doctrine of Satan and, on occasion, some principalities because it benefits them. Remember, Satan's kingdom was built on pride and lust, mainly the lust for power and greed, so his kingdom's climate will always be competitive.

The Rook

The rook can move any number of squares in any direction, horizontally or vertically. Second to the queen, they have a lot of mobility. For Satan, the rook is any principality in his kingdom. For God, the rook is the Holy Spirit. Both can move more freely than the bishops and the knights can. They also can work with the king in a move called castling. This will be discussed in the next chapter when discussing the movement of the king. The rook is one of the main pieces that gets the job done. They can do this because of their ability to have a lot of movement on the board. They are not as vulnerable as the queen; this is mainly because there are two instead of one, and their movements are slightly limited, but their powers are not to be underestimated.

The Bishop

The bishop can move forward or backward any number of squares, but only diago-

nally. The bishop is also very powerful and
still has authority, but within limits. For Satan, this would be his ministers, and for God,
this would be His ministers. While these ministers have authority, they can only move
where their father tells them to go. Most
people already know that God has ministered
in His Kingdom, mainly in the church build-
ings. Just as the bishop does for the king and
queen in the game, the ministers serve the
church and serve Christ. Pastoring, preaching,
and leading in worship are all acts of service.
Jesus demonstrated this when He came to
Earth as our Minister. He understood that He
was here to serve His Father and what would
soon be His church. Therefore, this is why He
washed the feet of all of His disciples, even
the ones who He knew would betray or deny
Him (John 13:5). But what about Satan's ministers? Well, they too perform acts of service. They serve him, the world, and his kingdom. These are not just ministers of satanic
movements, cults, and ministries, these are

also people who push Satan's doctrine and agenda. They could be celebrities who promote lust, violence, pride, and other forms of perversion. Even those who promote money-making tactics, but do not acknowledge Yahweh as their God, but instead make money their god are indirectly pushing Satan's doctrine. Satan's agenda is to keep God out of the equation. Though one may not be doing it intentionally, if one is pushing a message, has a following, be it small or large, and is not leading people to Christ Jesus, that person is only leading God's people to their spiritual demise.

Chapter 11

The Movements of the King

The king can move one square in any direction. The king may not be physically able to move in as many squares or as many directions as the other pieces on the board, but the king is the most important piece in the game. The king has the most influence, and every move that the other pieces make is based on the king's vulnerability, safety on their side and the ability to capture the king on their opponent's side. At the end of the day, it is all about the king.

As God's believers, we tend to forget that it is all about our King, Jesus. Yes, we have the gifts God has given us, we have the authority that God has given us, and we have a level of influence in the world, whether great or small. Angels are powerful, and they protect us and fight off dark spirits from Satan's kingdom. We have a certain level of reverence for our ministers who counsel us and pastor our churches, and rightfully so. But we must not lose sight of the fact that ultimately, it is all for Christ's sake. Every move that is made in God's Kingdom should be about Him.

Demons and principalities understand this as well. They too know that if they lose their king, they lose the game. They do not forget their purpose for being used by Satan. They work together to keep Satan's doctrine alive. Every move that is made in Satan's kingdom is intentional.

Castling

This is a move that is done with the rook and the king. The purpose of this move is so that the king can be in a safer position and away from the center of the board. This also helps the rook be in a more powerful position from the edge of the board to the center of the board. Essentially, the rook and the king are switching territories. This is only legal when they are in their original positions and the knight, bishop, and queen are not in between the king and the rook. The king moves two spaces toward the rook on the king's side of the board (short castle) or the king moves three squares toward the rook's position on the queen's side of the board (long castle), and the rook moves to the square that the king crossed.

Short Castle

A)

A short castle on the king's side of the board can only be done when there are no other pieces between the king and the rook.

C)

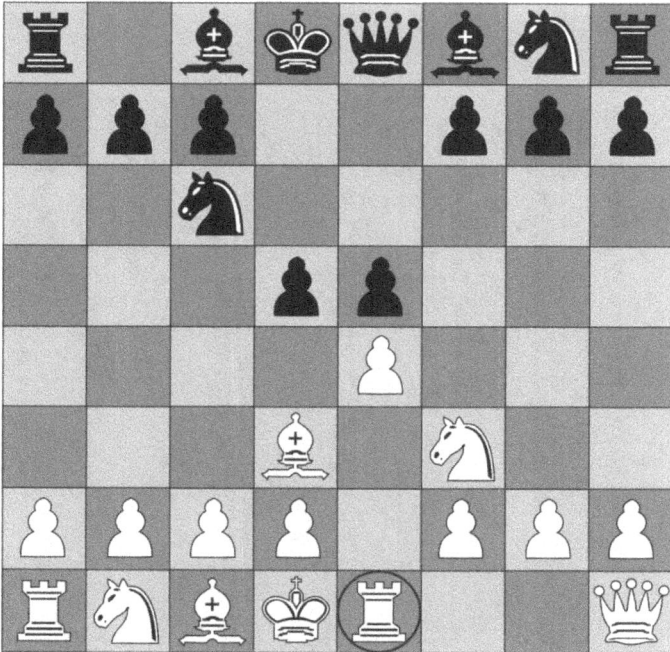

The rook has now switched places with the king and is now in a more active position to attack while the king is being protect-ed.

Long Castle

B)

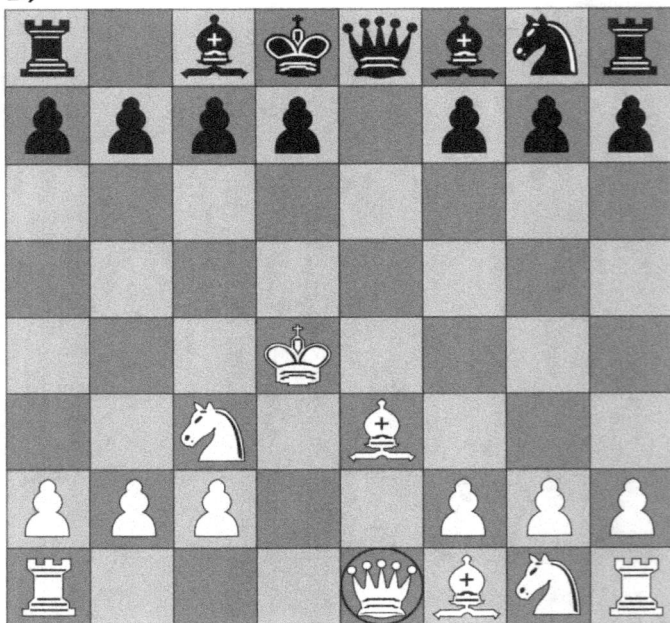

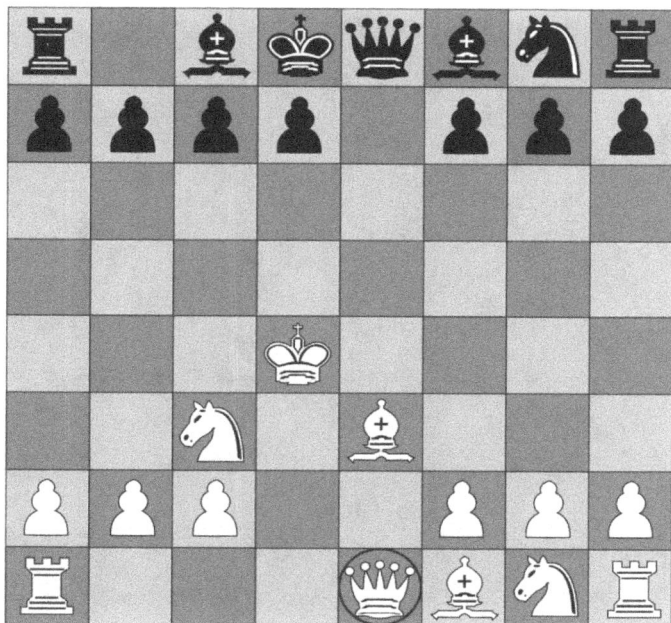

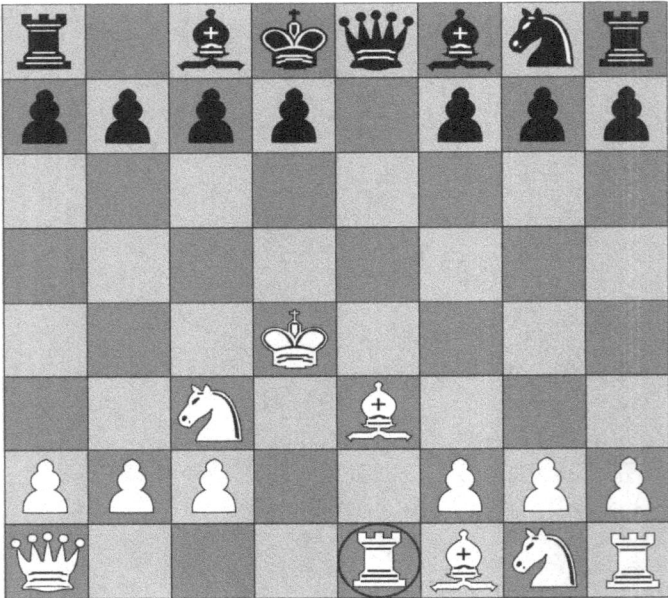

The king switches with the rook on the queen's side of the board. The same rules in a short castle apply to a long castle. This is called a long castle because the distance between the king and the rook is longer on the queen's side of the board (three squares) than it is on the king's side of the board (two squares).

Castling Regarding Principalities

Principalities will switch with their king to work with their king in spreading the doctrine of Satan. This puts the principality in a more active position. We see this in the book of Esther when Haman, the Agagite, was controlled by the spirit of lust (he lusted for the power) and the ability to be regarded as a god by all, especially by Mordecai, but Mordecai refused to bow to him (Esther 3:5). He made his way into King Ahasuerus' kingdom and used his position to manipulate the king into declaring a genocide on the Jews (Esther 3:8-14), God's children. This was a way of Satan using Haman as a rook so that his doctrine, his king, could be spread throughout the kingdom to attack God's people.

Castling Regarding the Holy Spirit

The Holy Spirit also takes part in castling; He castles with King Jesus. Jesus ascending to Heaven and sending down the Holy

Spirit (the rook) on the day of Pentecost was God making a castling move. Jesus is on the throne, protected, and not as vulnerable as He was when He was on Earth wrapped in human flesh. Now, of course, we know that Jesus is mighty and did not need protection. He could've freed Himself from the cross or avoided it altogether, but He did not avoid His destiny. This was in order to fulfill the prophecy and God's endgame. Nevertheless, this is still castling. Jesus' castling with the Holy Spirit has given us a greater advantage; it was a power move that allows Him to live inside us. Jesus could not move as much when He was walking on Earth as the Son of Man. But the Holy Spirit (the rook) is a way for God to have more mobility on the board while working with His queen, the church. Think about how the Holy Spirit moves, as demonstrated in the book of Acts, versus how Jesus Christ moved in the four gospels.

Chapter 12

The Center of Board

A commonly known fact in the game of chess is that the person who controls the center of the board controls the game. When you are in the center, you have the greatest ability to influence everything around you.

This is why Satan loves to control the media. As of right now, Satan and his principalities dominate the media. Media means middle, therefore, in the world, the media could be the equivalent of the center of a chessboard. Countless times, we see how easily influenced people are by the media. Once the tone of the media changes because of the news, Hollywood movies, and the most influential part of the media, the music industry, the climate of society changes; it always mirrors the media. The most powerful piece, the queen, is strongest in the center of the board, but is also at its most vulnerable position.

As of right now, Satan has his queen (pride) at the center of the board. When we follow the media today, we can see that pride is being pushed heavily. Examples of this are racial pride, patriotic pride, pride in our gender (feminism vs. male chauvinism), and pride in ourselves, the selfie generation. We also see that celebrities are even more prideful today than they were in the past. If you were to watch interviews and study celebrities in the past, typically before the early 2000s, they appeared to be more humble. There are many reasons why this is, but for this chapter, we will not explore this. Spiritually speaking, celebrities are now more boastful, and thanks to social media, they can give their pride a stage and have an audience 24/7.

We can also see that those who feed their pride always seem to want more attention. This is because pride, just like any other sin, is never satisfied. So, no matter how many Instagram likes, Facebook shares, or retweets one receives, that person will still want more. Pride is a beast that will keep growing and, as it gets bigger, will require more and more food.

But remember, as I mentioned before, the queen is the most vulnerable at the center of the board. So, when anyone who walks in pride is in the center, that person is more susceptible to being attacked for his or her speech, stance, or look. This has always been the case and is not right. Not everyone who is in the center walks in pride. But if you want to know who is truly walking in pride, pay attention to their responses. Typically, those who "clap back" are the main ones who walk in pride. Pride is an extremely vulnerable and insecure spirit. It needs constant validation and reassurance. When a critic does not feed it the food it likes, just like the beast it is, it roars. This is a common trait that we see in many of these new celebrities today. They engage too easily with people who are just fans and only dream about being in the positions they are in. This is what pride does. It gives you a high and haughty mindset but would quickly bring you down to the lowest level for the sake of protecting itself.

What if God's Queen Were in the Center of the Board?

Christians, just like any other human walking the Earth, have God-given gifts. God wants us to use these gifts to witness to others who may not know Him. Satan has no problem working his pawns overtime to lead people to hell. But those of us who say that we stand for God need to stop being afraid of being in the center of the board. Too many of us are comfortable with just burying our talents and hiding in the comfort of our own homes and churches. It is almost as if we want to keep Jesus for ourselves. Christianity is not a club. It is a lifestyle of love, peace, and sanctification. We must spread the gospel as it was our Messiah's desire for us to be fishers of men (Matthew 4:19).

It is the church's duty to evangelize and aim to influence others so that they can be led to Christ Jesus. Yes, it is true that as God's queen, we will be more vulnerable at the center of the board, but Jesus Christ, our King, was not afraid of being in the center when He walked this Earth. Similarly, He was at His most vulnerable, but He knew that our souls were at stake. Therefore, He did not abandon His responsibility for His own selfish desires. He had us in mind until His carnal death, and has kept us in mind even til this very day. We are running out of time, and if we do not work for God and fervently witness to the people in this world, their blood will be on our hands (Ezekiel 3:18). We do not have

the luxury of cowering or staying in our comfortable church homes. It is time to move.

Chapter 13

The Endgame

As I mentioned before, I did not know very much about chess at one point, and it was not until God gave me the inspiration to write this book that I started to study the game. I understood the general concept by then enough to start writing this book. But as I learned more, I continuously heard terms and chess jargon that I was unfamiliar with. I figured that the best way to learn was by playing the game. I was then led to research videos and audiobooks on chess. During my research, I came across this video on YouTube by Chess Audio Books entitled, "The Best Way To Learn Chess pt.1: This Advice Will Improve Your Game." One of the first things that this YouTuber mentioned was that the best way to learn chess is to know what your end game is.

He then mentioned that a lot of chess players, typically ones without coaches, tend to learn the openings first. Initially, I thought that it was rather counter-intuitive to learn the endgame first. Therefore, it shocked me when I heard the gentleman say that learning the openings first in chess is like learning chess backward. I was confused, but then I thought about it and realized that we do start almost everything with the endgame. For example, when we set goals, we start with our endgame. If you say to yourself, "I want to get a house by the end of next year," that is your goal and your endgame. Whether you realize it or not, you would then begin to work your plan out from there. I did not realize this at first because, like the average person, I typically do this quickly in my head. Your endgame is getting a house, so you then think about where the house will be and what price range you are looking for. Then you think about whether you will buy the house at full price or take out a mortgage. If you choose to take out a mortgage, you then think about how much you are willing to put as a down payment. But what you do not do is randomly decide that you are going to start working extra hours, take on a second or third job, and then randomly decide to purchase a house. When you are working towards a goal, you always know your endgame.

Even if it is just the near future, people without goals and visions have no endgame. So, these individuals go through life like beginner chess players who study openings before studying the different endgames. They work, and some of them even make a lot of money, but because they have no endgame, they squander their finances. Making a lot of money is not a goal, and if you see it as a goal, chances are, you have a scarcity mindset. But that is a topic to discuss in another book.

So, what is Satan's endgame? His goal is to have as many people as possible go to hell with him. But his endgame strategy is to separate you from God through sin. If he can entice you into sinning against God, then he can separate you from God. Sin is unholy, and God's Spirit cannot be around unholy things. Therefore, when Jesus bore all of our sins on the cross, He cried aloud, "My God, my God, why have you forsaken me?" (Matthew 27:46 NIV). Hell is an eternal separation from God. I believe that this is the pain that would be felt the most in hell. The heat will surely be tor-turous, but the eternal separation from God, the moving of God's hand from one's life for-ever, must be the deepest pain one could ever feel.

God's endgame is the exact opposite. God wants us to be with Him. The way God wants to use the church in the endgame is to have us bring people to Him. Our assignment is to witness and evangelize. Therefore, we must have an endgame that reflects us not only having God in our lives, but also testifies that we have brought other people to Christ.

Far too many people in the church seem to have forgotten what their endgames ought to be. Some believers have been deceived into believing that their endgame is to live a fulfilling and prosperous life here on Earth. While this is a beautiful thing to desire and is possible through Christ Jesus, it should not be an endgame for believers. As a matter of fact, for a believer of Christ, it is a given. Sure, we will suffer for His name's sake, and we will face being outcast and persecuted, but God will bless us in ways that we could not imagine. The endgame strategy for every believer should be, as stated before, to bring as many people to Christ as possible by doing the work of the Lord. This is bigger than us, and it is about more than just our desires. So, what is your endgame?

Chapter 14

Know Your Strengths, Weaknesses, and Capabilities

"If you know the enemy and know yourself, you need not fear the result of a hundred battles. If you know yourself but not the enemy, for every victory gained you will also suffer a defeat. If you know neither the enemy nor yourself, you will succumb in every battle."

-Sun Tzu *The Art of War*

It is important to know your strengths, weaknesses, and capabilities. If you are not aware of these things, you put yourself at a great disadvantage. As stated earlier in this book, one must always assume that their opponent is more than adept at the game of chess. Therefore, they must strategize a plan to defeat their opponent with the mindset that their opponent is a grandmaster. Our opponent, Satan, is indeed a grandmaster. He is a ruthless strategist who is not afraid to go in for the kill if the opportunity presents itself. He is aware of his strengths, weaknesses, and capabilities, just as he is aware of our strengths, weaknesses, and capabilities. Therefore, it is imperative that we have an awareness of these things as well.

Satan's Strengths

Satan's principalities are in influential positions in the world and have even made their way into our territory, the church. Yes, there are people in the church who are demonically influenced. They are in our territory to attack the church (the queen) and the reputation and influence of Jesus (the King). Another one of Satan's strengths is that he has control of the center of the board now, the media. Therefore, he has a significant influence on the game and a great advantage in the game. This may seem alarming to those who are not knowledgeable of the prophecy in the book of Revelation, which is currently being fulfilled, nevertheless, this is okay because it is a part of our Father's strategy. Pride is another strength that is his most powerful piece on the board, because it is at the center. There, it has the greatest influence on the world and on the church. Lastly, another one of Satan's strengths as a player is that he is a strategist and is skilled at analyzing his opponents and using their strengths, weaknesses, and capabilities against them.

Satan's Weaknesses

Pride, Satan's queen, is his most powerful piece, and although it is in a powerful position, it is also at its most vulnerable state. It is open and can easily be attacked. If we train ourselves to be spiritually aware, we can call out pride, along with other spirits that are blatantly showing themselves in the media. The principalities, Satan's rooks, are in our territory and can easily be attacked as well. We must recognize them when we see them manifesting in people in our churches, and then call them out either directly or in prayer. They will then be further exposed and can be cast out as well. The person who was once a piece for Satan can now be captured by God's Kingdom and can genuinely become a warrior for Jesus Christ while using his or her knowledge of Satan and his kingdom against him. Lastly, when Satan plays another strategist, he panics. He becomes reactive, tactical, and immediately goes on the defense. This is why he attacks believers who are in a vulnerable state, especially in their sleep through dreams and sleep paralysis. This is a defense mechanism against God and His plan. He also attacks us based on our capabilities of being able to destroy him. That is also an example of Satan being reactive or defensive. Thankfully for us, God is a better strategist. When Satan's skills and strategies are matched up against God's, he is the equivalent of an intermediate player, at best.

Satan's Capabilities

Satan can and will kill you if at all possible. If you allow him into your territory, he will seduce or bring you into his territory; if you go into agreement with him, you expose yourself to his attacks. He will use you to do his work, and then, he will destroy you. Be careful and stay submitted to God.

Our Strengths

A lot of us have been on Satan's team and have been one of his pawns. Therefore, we are familiar with his strategies and can strategize against him based on that knowledge. Another strength is that we are protected by God through His angels, the Holy Spirit, and the blood of Jesus Christ. Lastly, another one of our strengths is the gifts and talents that God gives to each of us like writing, creating music, singing and speaking in tongues. God has given us the ability to witness to those who do not yet know Him. Thankfully for us, our God is the ultimate strategist and we are on our way to victory if we stay in position and do not step out of order with God.

Our Weaknesses

We are humans who are wrapped in flesh. Therefore, there is a war within us between our spirits and our flesh. This makes us susceptible to falling into temptation. Another weakness can be not knowing God enough; this is regarding those who do not continue to learn and grow in Christ. If any of us do not seek God daily to learn about Him, what He wants for us, and who we are in Him, Satan can use our gifts against us. For example, a person who can easily connect with and lead people is most likely meant to lead believers in God's Kingdom in some way. However, if they do not receive this revelation from God because they have not spent enough time with Him or in His Word, Satan can use this gift against them. He would do this by attacking their finances and getting them into desperate situations to cause them to become con artists. A con artist understands people, can connect with people and lead people into believing and buying just about anything. If people with the gift of gab do not lean on God, they can be used for Satan's kingdom.

Many people who have the gift of creativity in music, writing, videography, and painting are meant to be used for God's Kingdom. But if Satan gets a hold of them and takes advantage of the fact that these people lack the knowledge and revelation they need to prosper in God, he can use them to minister to people in the secular world and spread his doctrine. Another way he attacks creatives is to get them bound by fantasy, just as he did to me. This can manifest through extreme daydreaming, unproductivity, and maladaptive daydreaming. Because I have struggled with this personally, I understand that all it simply means is that you have a great amount of creativity that you are suppressing. Get productive and turn your fantasies into a book that can glorify God. If your fantasies are not of God, renounce them. Submit yourself wholly and completely to God and resist Satan (James 4:7).

Maladaptive daydreaming is another form of spiritual bondage that falls in both the categories of fantasy and addiction. It is an addiction because you are aware that you are doing it, and you know that it is unsound, but you continue to do it because of the dopamine thrill you receive from it. It is typically birthed from an early life of traumatic events. Talk those events out with a therapist or counselor, preferably one who is saved and is familiar with this condition, as it is not well known in the study of psychiatry. If you cannot access these resources now, there are several YouTube videos that discuss trauma healing. I will have a list at the end of this book that you can refer to if you struggle with this. Do not believe the lie that Satan will tell, which is that "you are crazy." No, you are just bound and need deliverance. I don't suggest taking medication to suppress the urge to maladaptive daydream because this does not address its root cause. Address the root cause even if it hurts. Channel your creativity through a form of creative expression such as writing, music, or dance. Talk to God through prayer about your daydreams instead of talking to yourself. Your daydreams expose what is in your heart, and heart-to-heart conversations with God lead to confessions. Confessions lead to exposing spirits that are not of Him that may be influencing you, and once these spirits and ungodly things are exposed, make sure that you fast, pray, and go through deliverance. Lastly, anyone who struggles with any form of

bondage, drugs, alcohol, maladaptive daydreaming, and fornication, you must want to
be free. Once you are free, do not resubmit
to the things that God has now placed under-
neath your feet. You have dominion over
them. You have the authority to beat up and
bind the demons that have once kept you
bound. Know that this is your God-given
power; do not be afraid of it. Exercise wisdom
and stay away from your triggers, whatever
they are. For me, these triggers were movies,
tv shows, books, and music. I now understand
that I must constantly and continuously make
a conscious effort to be mindful of what I
consume. I made up in my heart not to go
back to what God delivered me from, but I did
not know what to do with my time other than
entertaining my triggers. I prayed to God and
confessed that I did not know how to be free
and I asked Him to show me how to be free.
From that day, God has kept me very busy
and I honestly do not even have the time to
be idle anymore. But He did not start trusting

me with assignments for His Kingdom until
He saw my willingness to be free from those
strongholds. You must want what God has for
you and be completely repulsed by what Satan has for you. This way, you are not put on
the defense, having to fight the temptation.
Instead, you can strategize on how to avoid
these traps altogether as much as possible.
We cannot always avoid Satan's attacks, but
sometimes, we go into his territory or to familiar places where we were once in bondage,
thinking that we are strong enough in our
flesh to resist the temptations. This is a foolish act; we must be wise. Understand that
Satan is terrified of God's church because of
our capabilities and the threat we pose to his
kingdom. So, he uses these tools of bondage
to keep potential warriors for God bound; this
is so that they would not rise against him.

Our Capabilities

We have the capability to break down
Satan's kingdom. We can do this through

evangelism, prayer, the casting out of devils, and by living our lives in a way that reflects the love and power of our Savior. If we study the Word of God while also being aware of Satan's attacks and we expose him for what he is and what he does, and if we stay in submission to God, we can annihilate him and his servants. We do this through the power of Christ Jesus.

The Good News

The best knowledge of all is that we will win. The good news is that the game is rigged, and God is the Creator of this game. So, while Satan may be a grandmaster, God is the Grandmaster of all grandmasters, and every move that has been made is all a part of His strategy and His divine plan. Rejoice, for it is already written!

A Warning

Jesus Christ is going to return to Earth, and He is coming for His disciples. He is coming back for those who believe in Him and have successfully held on to their faith, those who have finished the race. It is not definite when He will return, but it is most certainly going to be soon.

I listened to the book of Revelation for the first time when I was 19-years old. In the book, John writes that in his vision, people on Earth would worship an abomination. I asked myself how this was possible. How could anyone see an abomination and not flee from it, but instead worship it? Would it not be unnatural to our eyes? I did not receive my answer from God until I was 22-years old, and I listened to the book again. God revealed to me that the way that Satan is going to get people to worship this abomination is taking place right now. Every day, we are being desensitized to what is unnatural and ungodly. This is happening through the current trend of extreme plastic surgery, excessive piercings and tattoos (I have a tattoo and multiple ear piercings), extreme violence shown on television, blasphemy and profanity that is blatantly being expressed in media through movies and songs. Be prudent, vigilant, and do not entertain everything. Once people allow themselves to be desensitized to what is unnatural, they become accepting of these ungodly things. They would not even recognize that they are worshiping an abomination because they are being led by their flesh. Be careful. Jesus Christ will come like a thief in the night (Revelation 16:15, 1 Thessalonians 5:2) for those who do not keep watch for His return. We must remain watchful and on fire for our Father in Heaven. We must also be faithful, keep our lamps lit and not be like the five foolish virgins who were careless as stated in Jesus' parable in Matthew 25. Lastly, we must not be lukewarm like the church in Laodicea. Otherwise, He will vomit us out of His mouth (Revelation 3:16). Be prepared and stay on guard. I love you.

A Prayer For Salvation

If you are not currently saved and felt a calling from God while reading this book, do not waste any more time. Give your life to Jesus Christ now and make this declaration to Him:

Lord Jesus, I believe that You have died for all my sins. I receive You as my Lord and Savior. I acknowledge that You are the only Way, the Truth, and the Light. I repent of all my sins and ask for Your forgiveness. From this day forward, I give You complete control of my life. Not my will Lord, but Your will be done in my life, in Jesus' name. Amen.

If you have said this prayer and meant it wholeheartedly, you are starting a new life with Jesus Christ. Pray to God to lead you to a place for fellowship with other believers. Get baptized in water and the Holy Spirit in the name of Jesus Christ.

Welcome to the family!

Resources & References

List For Trauma Healing:

Forgiveness
- Anointed Fire- Forgiveness is NOT a process; It's a choice

Link: https://www.youtube.com/watch?v=XH9YWvMZkbQ

Rejection
🗁 **TED- What I learned from 100 days of rejection | Jia Jiang**

Link: https://www.youtube.com/watch?v=-vZXgApsPCQ

📄

📖 **Rose of Sharon- The Spirit of Rejection: My Story and Overcoming It**

Link: https://www.youtube.com/watch?v=odkLsSZS3Uo

📑 **Dephne Madyara- PRAYER AGAINST THE SPIRIT OF REJECTION**

Link: https://www.youtube.com/watch?
v=zN8qmfPbsAw
- Top Think- How to DESTROY Your
  Fear of Rejection
Link: https://www.youtube.com/watch?
v=be6com-qUIY

Maladaptive Daydreaming

- Ted Archive- Daydreaming: The bridge
  between imagining and creating |
  Aimee Mullins
Link: https://www.youtube.com/watch?
v=g_rKE_AWUWo

- Rafael Eliassen- How to Stop Day-
  dreaming | Start Visualising | Visual-
  ization Techniques
Link: https://www.youtube.com/watch?
v=F8imoM8dnqk

Sexual Abuse
- TEDx- Sexual abuse and rape can be
  the making, not the breaking of you |
  Lydia Ward | TEDxLeamingtonSpa

Link: https://www.youtube.com/watch?v=ehTtJRHlk-o
- Dig and Delve- Sexual Abuse and God's Healing Power - Lisa's Story

Link: https://www.youtube.com/watch?v=SqBqANkBWsE

- Sandals Church- Understanding God's Heart for the Abused | Sandals Church

Link: https://www.youtube.com/watch?v=oOoBNegwoDQ

Physical Abuse
- Harnessing Life- Healing From Physical Abuse | Harnessing Life

Link: https://www.youtube.com/watch?v=CBXltV_4GX4&t=22s

Narcissistic Abuse
- The Enlightened Target- 1st Step to HEAL from Narcissistic Abuse. Key Element to healing.

Link: https://www.youtube.com/watch?v=V9qiP6Z7WBo&t=169s

Divorce
- Katherine May- How to Deal with Parent's Divorce: My Experience + Tips | KATMAS 3

Link: https://www.youtube.com/watch?v=Can1SFzxWsE&t=29s

- Live On Purpose TV- How To Deal With Parents' Divorce In Your 20's

Link: https://www.youtube.com/watch?v=7cKzGkEuuaw

PTSD
- Complex PTSD Made Simple- Complex PTSD: Four Stages of Healing · Toxic Parents, Childhood Trauma

Link: https://www.youtube.com/watch?v=NSO-FluoHng&t=28s

▣ **Evangelist Fernando Perez- Healing Prayer: Trauma, Abuse, Rejection & Abandonment**

Link: https://www.youtube.com/watch?v=ESoeSz15_SM

- Evangelist Fernando Perez– Prayer for Healing Victims of Abuse – Prayer for Inner Healing

Link: https://www.youtube.com/watch?v=RVro3R6jLOI&t=29s

Bibliography

Baldwin, D. (2015, September 27). *Chess, Life & Strategy: A Discussion*. Retrieved from https://www.youtube.com/watch?v=lv6SpITq9E8

ChessAudioBooks. (2017, March 15). *The best way to learn Chess pt1: This advice will improve your game.* Retrieved from https://www.youtube.com/watch?v=3C-qTIx9J_jE&t=981s

Greater Minds. (2017, September 12). *What Is The Law of Attraction? Open Your Eyes To A World of Endless Possibilities.* Retrieved from https://www.thelawofattraction.com/what-is-the-law-of-attraction/

History.com Editors. (2019, December, 17). (2009, October 27). *History of Christmas.*

Retrieved from
https://www.history.com/topics/christmas/
history-of-christmas

History.com Editors. (2020, July 7). (2009,
November 18). *Halloween 2020.* Retrieved
from https://www.history.com/topics/hal-
loween/history-of-halloween

ADVEXONTV (2018) History Channel (2012).
The Origin of Halloween- Documentary. Retrieved from
https://www.youtube.com/watch?v=-
kxdGLpxIsU

History.com Editors. (2020, April 9). (2009,
October 27). *Easter 2021.* Retrieved from
https://www.history.com/topics/holidays/hi
story-of-easter

Lionel Giles, M.A. (1910). *Sun Tzu on The Art
of War: The Oldest Military Treatise In The
World.* London: Luzac&C. Retrieved from
*https://www.google.com/books/edition/Sun
_Tzŭ_on_the_Art_of_War/cpZQAAAAYAAJ?
hl=en&gbpv=1&printsec=frontcover*

Markushin, Y. (2014, August). *5 Most Typical Types of Chess Players (and how to beat them).* Retrieved from https://thechess-world.com/articles/general-information/5-most-typical-types-of-chess-player-s-and-how-to-play-against/

Rudd, S. *The Book of Judges: Samson.* Retrieved from https://www.bible.ca/archeolo-gy/bible-archeology-maps-conquest-time-line-chronology-judges-samson-philistines-1118-1078bc.htm

Valkanet, R., Discovery Bible., Biblos.com. (2010). *Bible Timeline* Retrieved from https://biblehub.com/timeline/old.htm

Images
Jaccard, S. *Sleipnir, Loki's son and Odin's 9-legged horse. Odin rode Sleipnir between worlds.* Retrieved from https://www.pinter-est.com/pin/515310382357706851/

McDermaid, B. (2019. November 7). *Wall Street's Charging Bull Sculpture is Moving.* Retrieved from https://www.cnbc.com/2019/11/07/wall-streets-charging-bull-sculpture-is-mov-ing.html

Vogel, N. *Santa and the Reindeer Riding Off Into the Sky.* Retrieved from https://www.pinterest.com/pin/42319769623 4157472/

All chess diagrams were created using the chess diagram setup on http://jinchess.com/chessboard/composer/